Aunt Mary's Guide

to Raising
the Old-Fashioned Way

AMY S. PEELE

To Megan —
All These Parenting
Tips Work!
Try Them
Amy S. Peele

Contents

The Chinese Gardens on Kale Island

Prologue

Reflections

"In the long run, we shape our lives, and we shape ourselves. And the process never ends until we die. And the choices we make are ultimately our responsibility."
—Eleanor Roosevelt

This collection of short stories reflects what I believe was a very common approach to raising children in the 1950s. Back then parents didn't give a kid a timeout. One good roar or a swift smack on the bottom got the immediate results they wanted. It is my belief that because of people like my Great Aunt Mary and my parents, there are many psychologists, psychiatrists, and therapists making solid livings and owning second homes today.

There are lessons to be learned from their creative approaches. It is up to the reader to be the judge. What I know is that my five siblings and I did not end up in a mental institution or federal prison. (Please knock on wood.) Every time we start to recollect a story in front of non-family members, silence and glances of disbelief ensue, followed by laughter. Those who have their own car keys usually don't stay for dessert or an after-dinner drink. The brave ones are still married to some of us.

There are stories that come out of my free and easy summers at Lake Wawasee in Indiana with Aunt Mary, and some from my sometimes-intense and painful days at home at 335 Indianwood. I now think Aunt Mary was just an easy, funny vehicle for me to discover and rediscover where my twisted coping strategies and practical values originated. My life was laced with love, happiness, struggle, violence, Irish humor, and the promise of relief from the cool summer waters of Lake Wawasee.

I survived a childhood with five independent, strong-willed, intelligent siblings from a "broken" home. My father left us in 1961 when I was eight years old. I was the fifth of the six kids, and my mother's mission was to keep all of us kids together, in Catholic schools, solely on the cash salary of her private-duty nursing jobs. She was, and still is, a devout Catholic, after two divorces and a third marriage that lasted over thirty years.

The memories and lessons we share created a bond

between us six kids that can never be broken. I most love those rare moments when several of us are together and someone starts to tell a story of our summers on Lake Wawasee at Kale Island. Each one of us listens, watching the storyteller to make sure all the details are accurately depicted.

To my intelligent siblings and mother, I say this: I'm writing what I remember from my childhood. How I processed the world from the age of six to twelve. If you have a different version of our life back then, I invite you to write it. We can sell our books in sets.

It doesn't take money to raise kids with proper manners, a hard work ethic, and no sense of entitlement. Provide freedom to children and allow them the room to exercise their imaginations and there's no limit to what they can accomplish. Many of the stories in this book reflect lessons that continue to serve me well to this day.

As with any memory, it's not what the memory does with you, but what you do with the memory that makes it either a useful lesson or an excuse not to do what you were put on this planet to do.

Mom and Dad, 1946

1

The Brothel

"Treat a lady like a whore and a whore like a lady."
—Milton Peele to son John, age 7

I was seven years old and did not know how to spell "brothel." It was a word I'd heard my parents use repeatedly when talking about my mother's Aunt Mary. I overheard my parents discussing her one evening when they were in the living room, down the hall from my bedroom.

"She has no tolerance for kids running around in her house. And that Bubs and Danny—they still wait on her hand and foot. I can't believe she bought them the house around the corner just because they ran that brothel for her.

They're waiting for her to kick the bucket so they can get all her money."

"Milt, if you hadn't gambled away the last three paychecks, we might be able to take the kids on a real vacation, like other families. Wouldn't it be nice to go to the land between the lakes in Kentucky or the Ozarks? We don't even have enough money for groceries this week. I had to call my mother and ask her to send me a check again. It's not like Aunt Mary has the brothel anymore. She cashed out and bought the Beacon. It's the best restaurant on Kale Island."

"It's the only one on the island. You can't count the root beer stand." Dad headed out our front door leaving Mom standing there hands on her hips. I knew it would be way past our bedtime by the time he got home coated with the smell of scotch and smoke, if he did come home at all.

If I'd asked my mom how to spell brothel, or any word, she would say, "Look it up in the dictionary. Don't expect people to just give you all the answers. Think for yourself." I often wondered how you were supposed to look up a word in the dictionary if you didn't know how to spell it, but it never stopped me from trying. The dictionary sat on the bookshelf above our family piano. Mom said her grandmother's dead body was inside the piano. That scared me enough to keep me from opening up the top. I went into the living room, took down the big book, and began my search by opening it to B, sounding out the word in my head. And then, there it was.

Brothel: house of prostitution

Prostitution: harlot

Harlot: prostitute

Just as I started to look up the word prostitute, I heard my mom call me to do my chores and so I put the dictionary back in its place. By the time all the dinner dishes were dried and put away, I had to pack my clothes for the early-morning drive to Lake Wawasee to see my grandma— we called her Mogi—and her sister, Aunt Mary, who lived next door to each other. This was our annual two-week summer vacation.

It was never hard to get up early to leave for the lake. All six of us would head out to the car, my father's voice listing our names in the order of our birth, "Bob, Charlene, Kerry, John, Amy, and Helen. Get in the car or we're leaving without you."

That morning, his large six-foot-four frame stood at the front door as we all herded into the turquoise station wagon parked in the driveway of our three-bedroom, one-bathroom home on the corner of Indianwood and Oswego in Park Forest, Illinois. Dad towered over Mom, who was five-foot-seven and slender. As she followed us out, he said, "Jesus Helen, we've been busy. How old are all these kids?"

"Let's see, Bob is thirteen, Char is twelve, Kerry is ten, John is nine, Amy is seven, and little Helen is four. Buckshot is four and Rebel is about one-and-a half."

"I don't care how old the collies are," my dad said as he lit his Pall Mall and backed the car out of the driveway.

Any cares I brought from home melted away as our car crossed over the bridge to Kale Island in Syracuse, Indiana.

The water from Lake Wawasee was the safest place in the world for me and was only a five-minute run from Mogi's house. The hot, humid days included long swims in the cool clear water, fishing, and thinking of creative ways to generate money for penny candy.

We could walk across the street to the Beacon and eat as much as we wanted, compared to home where food was almost rationed. After dinner there was no fight over who had to wash, dry, or put away the dishes—three very distinct tasks. The dishes really didn't need to be washed after the six

Peele children ate, especially after the fried chicken basket. If you hadn't witnessed us eat the chicken, you would have bet money it was picked clean by famished wild raccoons.

Among Aunt Mary's regulars were Bubs, Danny, Mogi, Grandpa Carl, and Froggy, all of whom also frequented her garage, where all the adult action took place. Most of our meals were prepared in Aunt Mary's renovated garage, which had a full kitchen and bathroom, and a sturdy round wooden table that sat eight. By day, my siblings and I went in and out of the garage for meals and check-ins. At the strike of five, however, the official cocktail hour began, which meant adults only until the dinner bell rang. Once it did, we swarmed in like locusts and consumed the hot, crispy fried fish that we'd caught and cleaned earlier that day under the tutelage of Mogi. After we had cleaned up the dinner mess, she only had to say two words, "Dairy Queen," and we would all cram into her big Buick for a much-anticipated Dilly Bar or a nickel cone dipped in chocolate.

After our ice cream treat, we would scatter to all parts of Kale Island to feed the swans at the Chinese gardens, catch fireflies, or sneak out for a forbidden midnight swim. The adults would linger and reconvene with full tumblers of scotch and soda, Pall Malls resting on the gigantic ceramic ashtray in the middle of the table, to commence their nightly ritual that included Canasta and local gossip.

Long after we were asleep in Mogi's white two-story house, the adults would swagger home by foot, or drive the short distance. Sometimes Aunt Mary would excuse herself early and walk the ten steps to her small yellow cottage and retire. She never entertained in her cottage; it was her private retreat.

"It's none of your goddamned business," she would respond if you ever asked her a question about anything— especially her home.

Our two-week vacation ended our summer, and on the last day Mogi would take the six of us to Pelcher's for new school shoes. I could count on this treat as sure as I could count on cocktail hour at five.

The fall after I turned seven, my dad had left our home in Park Forest for good. Mom grew a hard shell overnight and I could feel her anger from across the room. Mom had occasionally worked as a private-duty nurse when we needed to save up for something new, like a washer and dryer, but now she had to work fulltime just to cover the mortgage. Dad's gambling and partying had left our cupboards bare and the electricity and gas shut off more than once, but Mom, having to support the entire family on her own, took things to an entirely new level.

The nuns from St. Irenaeus, the Catholic elementary

school we all attended, had often summoned Mom to the principal's office and demanded to know when the back tuition payments would be paid. The new school year after my father left, however, shifted the landscape of our education. Aunt Mary agreed to pay for Catholic high school for Bob, Charlene, and Kerry since they were farther along. John, Helen, and I, on the other hand, were shifted from an education under the demon nuns to the kindness of public schools. I loved public school and the newness of it provided a distraction from the huge hole my father's departure caused in my heart. We were allowed to wear real clothes instead of the prison attire they called school uniforms. The school year flew by.

The summer following our first year of public school started like all the rest, with each of us waking up to a list of chores. It was made clear which room we were to clean and have checked by the oldest in charge. Once we were finished, we were free to spend the rest of our day at the Aqua Center. There were all shapes and sizes of pools there: adult only, toddler, wading, badge pool for those who could pass the test, and the teenage pool for when the coolness of adolescence finally found its way into you. I always got a severe sunburn the first day, as there was never any mention of sunscreen, only a race to see who got tanned first. Every year my mother came into my room the first night of summer to rub Dermassage, a lotion the hospital provided its patients, all over me. We had bottles of the stuff in our linen closet and she would apply this soothing white lotion to my skin and comfort me as I winced and moved past my first sunburn of the summer only to return to the Aqua Center the very next day to seek relief from the cool waters in the badge pool.

Summers at Lake Wawasee had made all of us excellent swimmers. Mom always told each of us, "When you were a baby I just threw you in and if you swam, great, and if not, well that was that." Nights at the Aqua Center were magical, swimming under the stars. Once they announced the pools were closed for the evening, slowly and reluctantly the water people would move across the cement floors to the locker rooms and out front to their parents' cars. Not us. "God gave us two good legs and they can take us anywhere we wanted to go," my mother declared any time we began to ask for a ride.

Some summer evenings she would meet us several blocks away from the Aqua Center at the Park Forest Plaza, which consisted of a collection of stores, restaurants, and the Holiday movie theatre. In the middle there was a grassy circle with a tall white clock tower. It was in this circle where I was introduced to my first licorice stick. This was nothing like the penny candy I'd been eating my whole life, but rather a musical licorice stick known as the clarinet. Big jazz bands would be set up right in front of Goldblatt's, our town's big department store. Not as fancy as Sears and nowhere near as elegant as Marshall Fields, Goldblatt's was where Maria, the famous store detective, worked. No one was supposed to know who the undercover store detective was, but everyone knew Maria. She didn't know she was the laughing stock of the town as she kept watch with her signature big black handbag clutched under her arm.

Music echoed from The Plaza as I walked toward it after the Aqua Center, with my wet hair and damp towel rolled under my arm. I would watch the adults enjoy the music and run around with the group of kids who were allowed to stay out late. Then we would go home with Mom, often falling asleep in the car, all our senses fully satisfied.

The summer after my father left, I was eight and there was no talk of going to Lake Wawasee. No talk about anything other than what bill would be paid that month. More than anything I needed to go to the lake and have my private conversations with it, under the water where no one else could hear. Why had Dad left us? What happened to our mother's smile? Why did all the people look down at us when we tried to cash Mom's second-party checks at the Jewel grocery store when that's the only way she got paid for her private-duty nursing jobs? Some of my friends' parents forbade them from playing with me because their parents said I was from a "divorced family." I never did go back and look up the word "prostitute." I didn't really care what it meant anymore.

Then one morning I heard the magic words, "Everyone get in the car—we're going to the lake." We never moved so quickly, throwing the bare essentials into bags and running to the car. The usual fight for the best seat didn't happen. Mom backed the station wagon out of 335 and we all began to recite the prayer to St. Christopher to give us a safe to trip to Lake Wawasee. Afterwards, we launched into a litany of sing-a-longs. Then, as if a timer had gone off, we all went quiet at the same time and listened to Mom as she started to tell us stories about when we were small. And this time she began with me.

Our Collie, Rebel

2

Pranksters

"Charlene stabbed him for real this time!"
—Little Helen

B efore I was born, my father moved a hospital bed into the living room for my mother, who suffered from the aftermath of her recently diagnosed polio. Apparently my mother wasn't in too much pain because that was the bed I was conceived in. Park Forest was a lower middle-class, planned community outside of Chicago. There were four Peele children back then—Bob, Charlene, Kerry, and John.

To hear my sister Charlene tell the story, I came into the family when things were great at our house. Dad had a job with a regular paycheck that he actually brought home, and we even had a maid, Carrie, who helped my mom run the house.

The story goes, when I was twelve days old, my brother Bob, then six, decided that there were too many kids in the house. He took me out of my crib, wrapped my pink blanket around me, and headed out the front door. He knocked on our next-door neighbors' front door and Mrs. McGovern answered.

"Why hello, Bobby, what's that in your arms?"

"It's my new sister, Amy. How would you like to buy her?"

"Well, how much do you want for her?"

"I don't really know, whatever you think."

"How about five dollars, would that be enough?"

Bob smiled, showing the wide gap between his front teeth, "Wow, that would be great!"

Mrs. McGovern went to get a five-dollar bill. When she came back, she handed it to Bob and he handed me over to her in exchange.

"Thanks Bob, you come see her any time you want."

Bob pushed his chest out and smiled as he walked back to our house. He picked up a basketball from the front yard and started to dribble it on the driveway. Several of his buddies came by on their bikes and invited him to a baseball game down the street.

My mother, meanwhile, was busy in the kitchen when Carrie came in inquiring about me.

"Where's Amy?'

Mom looked up from the sink, "She's sound asleep in her crib, but it's starting to feel like it's time for her to nurse."

Carrie gazed back at Mom, "That's what I was thinking. I went into check on her and she's not in her crib."

Mom raced past Carrie, wiping her hands on her apron. She ran back to the girls' bedroom to find an empty crib.

"Bob, Charlene, Kerry, John—where are you?"

"We're in the living room, Mom." She turned around and walked toward the living room where five-year-old Charlene was trying to show Kerry and John, three and two respectively, how to play Candyland.

"You know where your new little sister might be?" Charlene was already a great mother's helper and knew how to change my diapers and feed me.

Charlene glanced up with a confused look. "I saw Bob take her outside a little while ago," she responded.

"Did you see where he took her?"

"No, just out the front door."

My mother pushed the screen door open and was halfway down the driveway, yelling for Bob, by the time the door slammed shut behind her. There was no sign of him. As she started back toward the house, she heard someone call her name.

"Helen, I think I have something that belongs to you."

My mom turned around to see Mrs. McGovern holding me in her arms.

"Oh my God! How did you get her?"

"You'll have to ask Bobby. He's quite the little businessman." Mrs. McGovern chuckled and proceeded to tell my mother what happened.

Carrie came out to take me from my mother and brought me inside to change my diaper before feeding time.

Back in the house, my mother went into her bedroom and sat in the rocking chair until Carrie brought me in to nurse. My mother ran her fingers around my soft baby hair and checked the small bald spot right at the crown of my head. She had been alarmed when she first saw it after my birth. The doctor said to keep an eye on it, but that it was my birthmark and shouldn't be a problem. Once I got a little older, when my sisters started making fun of me for going bald, my mother scooped me up and whispered in my ear, "When you were born God put his thumb print on your head and said, 'You're a good one.'" After that, I was never self-conscious about my small bald spot because I knew the true story.

"Carrie," my mother said, "would you please find that boy? He needs to get home now. We're going to have a little talk."

Carrie walked outside, and just as she was ready to yell for Bob, he came riding up the street smiling. There was a white bag of candy hanging from his handlebars. Carrie looked at him and shook her head, "Robert John Peele, you get in the house immediately. Shame on you! Your mother is going to kill you."

Bob innocently looked up at her, "What'd I do?"

"You know darn well what you did—and what are you doing with all that candy? You know your mother doesn't allow you to eat that much. Where did you get that?"

Bob grabbed the bag tightly and let his bike fall sideways on the driveway before heading into the house. Carrie followed him inside. "Your mother wants to see you in her bedroom."

As he walked through the living room, Charlene, Kerry, and John looked up from their game. John's blue eyes locked onto the white bag and he screamed gleefully, "Candy! Candy!"

Bob ignored him, and forged on, only slowing down as he approached my parents' bedroom. He gently knocked on the door.

"Come in," my mother called out.

Bob walked in and stopped immediately when he saw the pink blanket over my mother's shoulder and me resting on her chest.

"You are in big trouble, mister. Just who do you think you are? How dare you take your new baby sister anywhere? What were you thinking?"

Bob watched my mother's face redden.

"I think we have too many kids and you don't have any time left for me. I don't think we need any more. Mrs. McGovern only has two kids, so I thought maybe she'd like another and we can always visit Amy 'cause she'll be living next door."

My mother took me off her breast, put me over her shoulder, and started to burp me. I let out a loud belch. "She's a Peele all right. Now, how could you even think about selling your sister?"

She turned me around to show Bob my face, breast milk dripping from my puckered lips. "Look how cute she is."

He looked at me and shrugged his shoulders. "We don't need any more kids, we're running out of room already. John and I have to share a room and Char and Kerry don't have any more room left in that little bedroom."

Mom looked down at the white bag he clutched in his hand. "What is that?"

"Candy."

"It looks like a lot of candy. Where did you get the money to buy it?"

"Mrs. McGovern gave it to me."

"That was certainly nice of her. I hope you did some chores for her."

Bob stood there as my mother put me on the other breast.

"You need to go next door and ask Mrs. McGovern how many chores you need to do to work off all that money. You know we don't accept money unless we earn it. Call your brother and sisters in here."

Bob leaned his head out into the hallway, "Char, Kerry, John, Mom wants you!" Then he started to back out the door.

"Bob, wait just a minute. I want you to stay here."

The three other kids came running into Mom and Dad's room.

"Yeah, Mom, what do you want?"

"I don't want anything, but your new little sister bought you all some candy and Bob is going to divide it up so that all three of you get the same amount."

"How did Amy buy candy, Mommy?" John asked. "She can't even walk." But his eyes were fixed on the white bag.

"You can ask your brother. You can each eat two pieces now and give the rest to Carrie to save for later. Bob, you go over to Mrs. McGovern's and be home in time for dinner."

As we got older, the incidents between my brothers and sisters and me got a little more intense. Growing up, my siblings were often going at each other—mostly Bob and Char and John and Kerry. There had been many near murders at 335, and my siblings were fond of threatening each other. Char often came after Bob with a butcher knife. Before our neighbor, Mr. Hay, died, he'd always been able to talk her down and get the knife back before she actually committed a crime. It didn't help that Bob never stopped laughing at Char the entire time she was threatening him.

I don't think anyone can tease quite like a Peele. It was a fine art of protection we learned early on in order to survive at 335. It was a craft that required two drops of pure brutal honesty, mixed with six drops of humor, a straight face, and finished with a quick but deep belly laugh.

One time we pretended Bob had been killed in the kitchen. Little Helen was young enough to believe that the catsup we'd poured on him was real blood. We convinced her that we had to drag him out into the backyard and bury him before Mom got home or she would kill us. She cried and helped us move his long body out the back door. We started digging the hole and asked Helen to be the lookout for Mom's car. Not more than several shovels of dirt latter, Mom pulled into the driveway, her headlights illuminating our scarcely furnished living room.

Helen screamed, "She's home! She's home!" Mom got out of the car in her dirty white nursing uniform, looking exhausted. Helen ran up to her and hugged her. When Mom bent down to hug Helen back, Helen started sobbing. By this time, I'd made my way to the living room and I could see that Mom knew something was going on. She looked up past her hug with her "I know they're up to something" look. Mom whispered something into Helen's ear and Helen whispered something back. We hadn't taught Helen how to lie yet. Mom stood up and hand in hand with Helen walked around the side of the house to the backyard. There, leaning up against the back door, were three shovels of various sizes. There was a long shallow hole dug in the middle of the backyard, no children in sight. Mom opened the back door with Helen still in tow.

"Alright you kids, get in the kitchen now!" John and my older sisters slowly started to file out of the bedrooms, and I emerged from where I'd been standing in the living room. Each of us wore our most relaxed, nothing's happening face. I looked up and saw my mother's tired and thin face. She had worked fourteen hours.

"Where's Bob?" Char, Kerry, John, and I turned as if he were about to come around the corner, but Helen spoke up. "He's dead, Mom. He had blood all over him and we had to bury him in the back yard." She burst into tears again. "Charlene stabbed him for real this time!"

I was biting the side of my mouth so I wouldn't laugh out loud. It was hard to tell if my mother was in a mean tired mood or a good sense of humor mood. Just then Bob walked in through the back door and Helen ran up to him and hugged him. He looked up at our mom with his innocent brown eyes. "Hi Mom, how was work?"

"My day was just fine. Got blood all over me from my patient. Looks like you got a little blood on you too. Did you cut your chest?"

Bob started to smile and checked Mom's reaction before giving it his full gappy toothed, dimpled smile.

"Shame on you kids for scaring Little Helen. She's only four years old. Now each one of you apologize and don't do that again. Wipe up that catsup off the kitchen floor and Bob, you go out in back and fill in that hole." One by one we muttered our insincere apology and left the kitchen.

The older we got the more sophisticated our teasing and pranks evolved, sometimes out of control and sometimes providing the comic relief we needed to survive.

Mogi and Gogi

3

Mogi and Aunt Mary

"Aunt Mary had one of the biggest butts I had ever seen in my entire eight years."

—Amy

I remember looking up into her crystal blue eyes. She wore glasses, but I didn't see them. Her eyes penetrated mine in a gentle, focused way, as if exploring my soul. I wasn't afraid to let her see what I was like inside, if she had that power. I always thought she did. I was eight, and she was my grandmother. We called her Mogi because when Bob, the oldest, tried to say Grandmother, "Mogi" is what came out—and when he tried to say Grandfather, "Gogi" was all he could say. Gogi was not Mom's biological dad—and he was Jewish, though I didn't know what that meant at the time.

Mogi sat at the round cranberry-colored Formica table. I stood in front of her, our eyes at the same level. Her light brown hair was curled tight, still covered by the hairnet she wore to bed each night. She wore a flowered cotton housecoat that came to just below her knees as she stood up to pour herself another cup of coffee. Her blue fabric house slippers matched her housecoat. She was tall and thin, and she didn't have a big butt like her sister, Mary.

It was my first full day of vacation at Lake Wawasee that year, the summer after my father had left, and I was the first one up, dressed in a pair of blue cotton shorts and a sleeveless white short top, hand-me-downs from Kerry. My clothes hung loosely on my tall, thin body.

The months leading up to Lake Wawasee that year had been filled with sadness, fear, and confusion. It was as if the mercury in the thermometer Mom put in our mouth when we were sick was going to blow out the top. Dad left the house crying with just one suitcase. Helen and I started to cry as we watched him drive away. We didn't understand why—why he was leaving, why he'd cut himself out of all the family photos, and why he and Mom yelled such mean things at each other.

As the station wagon sailed down Route 30 that summer, I could feel myself start to get more comfortable, like it was all right to really sit in the car and even lean back and relax. I knew relief was not far away. First the truck stop for our usual milkshake and potty break and then the cool waters and long lazy afternoons at Lake Wawasee. It would be different without Dad, but I couldn't wait to get there anyway. As we passed the Dairy Queen, we all agreed that our first mission would be to rip off our clothes, put on our suits, and run straight to the lake. We barely gave Mogi a hug. Her eyebrows seemed lower on her forehead than usual, and she seemed softer in spirit than the previous summer. I guess she must have wanted to cut us all some slack because she didn't even make us pick up our clothes. Now it was the next morning, and I sat alone with my grandparents at the kitchen table itching to get down to the lake. I ran my fingers through my summertime pixie haircut, waiting for the perfect moment.

I looked at Mogi, "Mogi, can I run down and say hi to the lake?" I asked.

She glanced up from her morning paper. "You know it's too early to swim."

"I just want to see if the shells I left under the bench are still there."

"All right. You know not to go near the water. We'll be having breakfast soon, so don't be long."

I nodded and leaned over and kissed Mogi's soft cheek. The smell of coffee drifted from her pale thin lips. She picked up her coffee cup with her long fingers. Her hands looked old with their brown sunspots and she wore a sparkly diamond ring she'd gotten a long time ago from Gogi.

As I walked out the back door, Mogi lit up a cigarette. The day before I had swum as fast and as far as I could, leaving the icky feelings and memories from Park Forest far behind me. I took my first long underwater dive and pulled up a handful of sand mixed with shells and rocks that sparkled in the sun, evidence that summer was here and so was Lake Wawasee. I left everything I'd collected in its usual place. I raced down the gravel driveway in my bare feet. I wasn't looking down, and I stubbed my big toe on a jagged rock. It started to sting. I stopped and pulled my leg up to look at the damage. It was bleeding freely, and a flap of skin hung from my toe. I decided to rinse it in the lake. It wasn't a big deal. It wouldn't be summer if I didn't stub my toe.

It took about five minutes to run to the lake. Everyone's morning papers were still outside their houses. As I turned into the grassy area in front of the lake, I stopped in front of the tall white pole with a white birdhouse on top. A sign stated that this was Kale Beach, a private beach for the following families only. The list of names included my grandparents, John and Lillian Kurtzfield.

I could hear the steady pace of the soft waves hitting the cement wall before I could actually see the calm waters of Lake Wawasee. The clean smell of the water and air filled my lungs as I took in a big, deep breath.

It was about twenty feet from the road to the water. Grass interspersed with gravel covered the ground between the road and the white pier.

In front of the lake was the white painted bench, which sat empty, facing the lake as always. Sure enough, my rocks and shells were still safely under it. I was happy no one had stolen them.

By now my toe was really starting to sting. At the end of the pier, I sat down and dipped my feet into the cold lake water. The chill of it sent shivers throughout my body, and a pleasant numbness set in my feet. I wiggled my toes around, and used my hand to rinse small pieces of gravel out of my stubbed toe. I knew that the water would do the rest of the healing, as it had every summer before.

I looked out over the huge lake, excited about the prospect of swimming in it all day. As I looked down, I could see all the new rocks and shells waiting for my brothers, sisters, and me. The sound of waves softly hitting the seawall sent me into a peaceful trance until the quacking of a mother duck and her ducklings interrupted my daydream. I hopped up, wondering how long I had been sitting there. As I went to smooth out my shorts, I noticed that I was damp from the morning dew on the pier. I hoped Mogi wouldn't notice. I grabbed my stones and shells and started back to the house. Before I walked in through the back door, I saw that my toe had stopped bleeding.

The smell of toast permeated the kitchen. Mogi looked up at me.

"Outside!"

I stopped in my tracks—there was no way she could have seen my wet shorts.

"Leave the rocks and shells outside. None of that in my house."

Relieved she wasn't angry, I backed down the two steps. I walked around the side of the house and found a spot where I could hide them.

On my way back in, before the back door had even closed behind me, Mogi began, "Wash your hands and sit down. Gogi made your favorite."

During the time I was gone, she had gotten dressed in a pink cotton V-neck ironed blouse, tucked neatly into a pair of dark cotton slacks. She had on her old lady shoes, tan leather with ties in the front. She said she wore them because they were comfortable and good for her feet. She had identical pairs in black, white, and brown.

I slid into one of the kitchen chairs. None of my brothers or sisters were up yet. It was just Mogi, Gogi, and me. Gogi stood over the stove with his white-ribbed T-shirt tucked into his trousers. My mother told me that he kept small diamonds sewn into the lining of one of his pockets, a habit he brought over from the old country. His thick black and white hair was neatly combed back from his forehead with the help of Brylcreem—"a little dab'll do ya." Black framed glasses covered his deep-set brown eyes, his bushy eyebrows showed just above the rims. He grinned at me with his thick, well-trimmed moustache smile.

"You ready for your special breakfast?"

"Yes, please."

He placed in front of me a bowl with a poached egg and a piece of buttered toast broken up so the toast could soak up the runny yellow yoke. Gogi added just a pinch of salt and pepper, patted me on the shoulder, and sat next to Mogi. I enjoyed the warm, crunchy breakfast treat, and quietly watched Mogi and Gogi settle into their morning ritual. Mogi looked over at me and said, "You kids better behave while you're down here. Your Aunt Mary likes her peace and quiet." I smiled and gulped my last sip of milk. I did not want to make Aunt Mary mad.

My mind wandered back to the conversation between my Mom and Charlene in the car the afternoon before. Charlene was sitting next to Mom in the front seat.

"When we get to the lake, keep a sharp eye on little Helen and Amy," Mom said, keeping her eye on the road as she drove. From the back seat of the station wagon, I could see Charlene's chubby-cheeked profile as she turned her head toward Mom.

"I usually do. Why, is there something wrong?" At twelve, Charlene had become like our second mother, especially to Helen, who was just four-and-a-half.

"Don't you remember what Aunt Mary did to you when you were five?"

Charlene looked up at Mom, her eyebrows pushed together, "No."

"You and Aunt Mary locked horns, and she won. She asked you repeatedly to go into Mogi's house for your nap.

You were the size of a three-year-old, but you had the temper of a grown man. You stamped your feet and cried that you were not tired and that you wanted to go swimming. You wouldn't stop. Without a word, Aunt Mary picked you up, carried you over to the clothesline, took some wooden clothespins, and pinned you and your ruffled dress to the line. She walked back into her house and left you hanging there, wailing." Charlene remained silent for so long that the rest of us decided to change the subject by singing all the verses to "She'll Be Coming Around the Mountain."

I was brought back to Mogi's kitchen by Gogi's deep voice, "Amy, clear your place and go get your lazy brothers and sisters up. It's nearly nine."

I put my dishes into the sink of hot soapy water that Mogi had already drawn, and ran around the house, yelling, "Last one to the lake is a rotten egg!"

One by one, my brothers and sisters got up, used the bathroom, and wandered into the warm kitchen.

"There's cereal, bananas, and juice on the table. If you want toast, help yourself," Mogi directed. "Don't go upstairs waking your mother. She needs some time alone."

It was the first time Mogi didn't have tenants upstairs, so Mom had her own private apartment.

After everyone finished eating, Mogi came into the kitchen. "You have to wait an hour before swimming, so make your beds, put your suits on, and then you're going to go say hi to your Aunt Mary. But she doesn't want to be bothered until at least ten, so don't go over there until I say."

We decided to kill time by going into the living room and playing games. The six of us were like a pack of racing horses waiting for Mogi's voice to signal the dash to the lake—and finally it came.

"It's ten thirty, you all can go swimming now!" she announced. We started for the front door. The horses were out of the starting gate.

We were halted by Mogi's voice. "You children need to pick up these cards and games and put them away," she called out. "I'll not have you leaving a mess in my house."

We quickly shoved every marble back into the Parcheesi box, and the cards neatly into their case, and then resumed our stampede out the door.

"Don't forget!" Mogi said, thwarting our attempt once again. "Go over to Aunt Mary's house and say good morning to her. I'll come down to the lake to get you when it's time for lunch."

There was a collective sigh as we slowed our pace and headed toward Aunt Mary's. I was afraid to go into her house. I didn't want to get her mad. Overhearing our quiet complaints, Mogi hollered after us, "I'll have none of that! She's my only living sister, and she's been very generous to all of you."

Bob pushed his way in front and led us to Aunt Mary's. He knocked on her screen door, barely waiting for her flat, raspy "Come on in." Aunt Mary was sitting in her big, brown Lazyboy chair, still in her housecoat. She smiled slightly when she saw Bob, her favorite, leading us in.

We filled up Aunt Mary's small, fancy living room pretty easily. Her long gold couch was covered with plastic that squeaked and made fart noises when we sat on it. Her business desk was facing out toward the window. Everything in its proper place.

"Hi, Aunt Mary," Bob grinned.

"I can see where you're all heading. Did Mogi make you come over?" She ran her long fingers over her thick black hair, touching the neatly braided circle in the back.

Bob lied for the group. "No, we just wanted to say hello."

She took a long drag off her Pall Mall and slowly blew the smoke out toward us. She put her cigarette out in her gigantic orange and red ceramic ashtray. She wore black glasses with sparkling stones at the tips. They could have been diamonds, but no one asked.

"Your grandmother has been talking about your visit for weeks, she's so excited. I've got a little something for each of you, if you can just wait a minute."

She grabbed the wooden handle on the side of her chair, and let the foot bar slide down and under. She stood up, towering over us with her six-foot frame. Her large breasts were all I could see when I looked up. "I'll be right back."

We watched her walk through the short hallway to her bedroom. From behind, her long skinny legs disappeared where they collided with what had to be one of the biggest butts I had ever seen in my entire eight years. We dared not laugh. She returned with her black leather handbag, and backed herself back into her chair.

We inched our way toward her.

"Move back, there's enough for everyone." We reversed a few steps.

She reached into her handbag, pulled out her black silk coin purse, and unsnapped the metal clasp.

"Here's a quarter for each of you. After lunch, you can go down to the root beer stand and get whatever you want." She studied each of us as she put the quarters into our palms. I looked up into her clear blue eyes and closed my fingers around my loot. A whole quarter, all for myself. I was rich.

"Thanks, Aunt Mary."

"You kids stick together, and be careful in the lake. Don't bother Froggy and he won't bother you."

Froggy owned the house next to our beach, and depending on how many beers he drank, he was either really nice, or really loud.

We hurried down the gravel road toward the lake, talking over each other about how we were going to spend the money. Char walked slowly behind us, carrying the big black truck tire inner tube that we played with in the water.

Up ahead, I saw Bob and John sticking their butts out as far as they would go, spreading their legs, walking with their legs as far apart as they would be if they were riding a horse, and laughing. Kerry turned around and looked at Helen and me, "Time for your best Aunt Mary big-butt impression."

We slowed down our pace, jutted our butts out, spread our feet wide, and wobbled as we moved forward, laughing the rest of the way. Once we got to the lake, we carefully laid out our towels on the white bench, each of us wrapping our quarters into the corner of them.

Bob and John ran the length of the pier and cannon-balled in. Helen and I went down the ladder in the shallow part and eased our way into the cool water. It was just after ten thirty, so the sun wasn't hot enough for a fast dive in just yet. Kerry went to the end of the pier, and before she could get in, Bob and John started to splash her, so she jumped in and swam after John, because she knew she could push him under. Bob came to his rescue, and both boys splashed Kerry. She took a long dive under and started to swim out toward the white raft in the deeper part of the lake.

The rest of the morning disappeared as we swam under the pier and collected shells and pretty colored rocks. Kerry, Bob, and John played King of the Raft. Char finally got in the water, and Helen and I joined her on the big inner tube, making it bounce back and forth until one of us fell off laughing.

There were occasional big black horse fly alerts, forcing us all under the pier for fear of being bitten.

"Okay, out of the water! It's time for lunch!" Mogi yelled out. She stood there smiling for a little while before slowly turning around to make her way back to the house. We all raced to the nearest ladder, grabbed our towels and quarters, and followed her. Lunch at Mogi's was always a treat.

After lunch, it was right back to the water. The afternoon sped by and we didn't get out until the sun started to go down. We never talked about what was happening at home as we swam under the pier and chased each other. We got out of the water reluctantly, and straggled back to Mogi's house relaxed, hungry, and happy. As we got closer, we could hear the voices of Mom, Mogi, and Aunt Mary coming from Aunt Mary's garage. I walked in behind Kerry. Aunt Mary was sipping her scotch on the rocks, her lit cigarette hanging on the edge of her huge ashtray waiting its turn. Aunt Mary looked up as we piled into her garage. Her raspy voice began, "I'm sure you kids are in here sniffing around for dinner. We're giving your mother the night off. You get yourselves cleaned up and I'll take you all over to the Beacon for dinner."

We raced to Mogi's house and kept the shower going as we each jumped in and out. Going to the Beacon was quite a treat, since we had just the basics at home—and not a lot at that. A half a banana with cereal at breakfast and seconds were rare. We ate healthy, but in limited amounts.

Since Aunt Mary owned the Beacon, we could order whatever we wanted, which was usually a cheeseburger or a fried chicken basket with fries. I felt like a princess as the waitress took my order and gave me as much root beer as I could drink. After we were finished, there were only chicken bones left in the baskets and not even a single French fry left. We got to just sit there as the waitress cleaned up. I even had dessert: ice cream with chocolate sauce. I felt like the richest girl on all of Kale Island. To top it off, there were no dishes and no fighting over whose turn it was to dry and put them away.

One by one we thanked our Aunt Mary for dinner and walked outside to bursts of lights sparkling in the warm night air. The fireflies were inviting us to catch them. I never thought about home when I was at Lake Wawasee, I was in a different world where there with no worries or pressure. For two weeks each summer we got to live a different life: abundant food and total freedom. It was nourishment for our souls and our bodies.

Helen and Amy

4

Oil Cloth

"Hey, mummy arms."
—Bob

I was hospitalized for bronchial asthma several times when I was in the first and second grades. One day, when I was seven-and-a-half and having an asthma attack, my mother slapped my face and told me I was not going to have asthma anymore. Being a compliant child, I didn't.

Several months later, my hands and wrists began to itch and I scratched them all the time. Mom and Dad thought I was allergic to the varnish on the desks in Mrs. Oakley's third grade class at St. Irenaeus. What a dumb name for a saint. All the kids in the neighborhood who didn't go there always made fun of us, shouting, "Saint who is an ass!" It was funny at first.

I didn't know it at the time, but the asthma and then my rash were my body's way of communicating my fear and sadness about what was going on in our house.

Mom and Dad were fighting a lot, and Dad would come home drunk late at night. I remember Mom helping him to the bathroom, asking him, "Where's the paycheck, Milt?"

I believed my parents' theory about the desks, but I couldn't understand why, all of a sudden, the same desks I'd been sitting in throughout first and second grade would now cause this terrible rash.

Then the itch began on the inside of my elbows and at my wrists and both arms. During the night in my sleep I would scratch so hard that I would wake up with red scabs and dried blood that caused my pajamas to stick to my arms. It slowly started to take over both my arms, and then my palms, and then my hands. Every night, I would dig in my sleep to scratch this terrible itch. My scratching never seemed to wake up Helen, who shared a twin bed with me at the time.

The rash got so bad that Mom had to wrap me in elastic ace bandages that wound all around my arms and fastened the end with a small metal prong. Some nights that worked, but some mornings I would wake up with the bandages unraveled and my skin raw and oozing. The itch was so bad that I would rub my hands and do anything I could to try and stop it.

One weekend morning, I sat on the top bunk of my brother's bed with my brothers, sisters, and parents around me, all trying to analyze my rash. Dad brought in some Desenex that he and my brothers used for their athlete's foot. He spread some on my wrist and I started to scream and cry. It felt like someone had put a hot match to my skin and it kept burning and burning. My dad looked at John and said, "Quick, go and get a warm washcloth so we can wash it off." John ran across the hall, came back, and tossed the washcloth to my dad. He gently wiped off the medicine, as tears streamed down my face.

Mom looked at my wrist, "Looks worse than before, Milt. Go fill a bucket with warm water and a cap full of bleach, and put it on the kitchen table on a towel. She's going to have to soak first." My dad left the room, and my brother helped me hop down from the top bunk. I walked into the kitchen, where Mom and Dad were standing next to the bucket.

"Amy, I want you to soak your hands in here. It'll sting a little at first, but then it'll feel good."

I was scared, but I slowly immersed my hands. There was an instant sting, then just the feeling of warm water and tingling. It was a relief after the Desenex. My hands started to itch, so I made sure no one was watching before I rubbed them together in the warm water, enough to soothe the itch. After twenty minutes, Mom came into the kitchen, and put a towel and tweezers down on the table.

"Take your hands out, honey, and let me dry them." My skin looked like raw red meat. The top layer of my skin was mostly off my hands, wrists, and inner arms. She examined them closely. "I'm going to have to debrede them. It won't hurt. I have to get the dead skin off so the new skin can breathe and come in. Now, put both your hands on the towel. This is how they treat bad burns at the hospital."

I looked at her. "Are you sure it won't hurt?"

"I promise, the skin is already dead, it just needs to come off."

She sat across from me, and started to carefully take the loose white pieces of skin off my right hand with the tweezers. It didn't hurt, but my hands still itched.

"My hands itch, Mom. It's so hard not to scratch."

"Itching is a sign that the skin is healing, but if you keep scratching, you won't be able to heal. Just put pressure on the places it itches, don't rub or scratch."

Easy for her to say. After she got through debreding both hands, wrists, and arms, she put some A&D ointment on them and then wrapped the ace bandage from my fingers up past my elbows. Then Bob came in to get something to eat out of the icebox.

"Hey, mummy arms."

Mom looked up at him. "Get out of the icebox. Dinner will be ready soon enough. Amy, empty the bucket out into the bathtub and rinse it out. We'll need to do this every day until this clears up."

After dinner, Mom looked over at Kerry and said, "You'll have to do Amy's dish duty tonight, and the rest of you will have to take turns until she heals."

My siblings clicked loud noises with their tongues and groaned as they cleared their dishes from the table, giving me their best evil eyes when Mom and Dad weren't watching. I felt mad at them for resenting me and for this awful thing I had to deal with.

The next morning, Mom came in to get us up for school. "Come on, girls. Time to get up. Amy, let me see your arms." When Helen got up to pee, I scooted to the edge of the bed and held out my arms. "See Mom, I didn't scratch last night. Maybe they're all better."

My mother started to carefully take off the bandages. As she got to the final layer close to the skin, the bandages were stuck to my arms.

"We'll have to put some warm water on the bandages to loosen them. Sometimes the oozing from the skin makes the bandages stick, and we don't want to just pull them off. Let's go into the bathroom." As we walked out of the bedroom Mom directed my sisters to get breakfast on the table. "Char, there's oatmeal on the stove, and Kerry, you make the toast." I followed Mom into the bathroom.

She was able to get the bandages off with the water, and then I had to get ready for school. I went in and put on a short sleeve white cotton button-down shirt and red plaid pleated skirt, my school uniform. I put on my white socks and black tie shoes. My hands felt stiff and looked puffy. I felt so ugly as I sat down at the kitchen table and started to eat my breakfast.

Kerry looked across at me. "Looks like you have some bad disease. We'll call you *disease* from now on. *Disease! Disease!*"

Mom came into the kitchen. "Amy, come back here so I can put some more medicine on your arms and bandage them before you leave for school."

I was horrified as I walked back to the bathroom. "I can't wear those bandages to school. All the kids will make fun of me. Please don't make me. Please"

My mother got out the A&D ointment. "You go to school to learn. It's nobody's business what's on your arms or hands. I'll wrap the bandages so you can still write. Everything will be healed before you know it."

She wrapped my arms and part of my hands. "Now, go get your coat on, and get to school before you get a tardy."

I left the house with John and Kerry and we walked the mile to school. Kerry got in a few more "*disease*" shouts before we got there. The bell rang and we all lined up in our respective classes and marched quietly to the lockers right outside our classrooms. Everyone took off their coats, except me. I was able to get to my seat by the window quickly, hoping Mrs. Oakley wouldn't notice that I still had my coat on. After roll call, she looked back at me. "Amy, please put your coat in your locker."

When I didn't move, she started walking toward me. You never disobeyed Mrs. Oakley. She was one of the meanest teachers at St. Irenaeus.

She came close to my face. "Are you cold? We can turn up the heat. You can't get your work done with that parka on. Now follow me, and let's put your coat in your locker."

I followed her out into the hall. "I don't want to take my coat off, I'm really cold."

"Miss Peele, take your coat off now, or you're going to the principal's office!"

I prayed that no one would see me out in the hall as I took off my coat and watched Mrs. Oakley stare at my bandaged arms.

"What happened? Did you burn yourself? Is there a note from your mother?"

I just looked at her, totally humiliated. Several students from different classes slowed to stare at me as they walked their class attendance slips down to the main office. I felt like a freak. Just then, Sister Mary Jane came down the hall and stopped. "What seems to be the problem here?" She looked at Mrs. Oakley, and then at me, and then my arms.

I started to cry, I was so embarrassed. "I have a bad rash, and until it gets better I have to wear these bandages to school. Please don't make me take off my coat."

Sister Mary Jane looked at Mrs. Oakley. "I guess it will be okay for today, but tomorrow bring your navy blue sweater. We have a dress code here."

I kept my jacket on for the rest of the day, and none of my friends asked why. We were too busy playing and talking. For the next several days, I went through the soaking, debredement, and wrapping. My sweater didn't cover up the bandages as well as my coat, but I told my two best friends, Martha Ward and Chris Welch, that I burned myself, and they never asked me any other questions.

Finally, everything healed well enough that I didn't have to wear the bandages any longer. I still had the rash on my hands and wrists in some places, but that was nothing.

Once I'd healed, my mother came with me to see Mrs. Oakley before school. Mrs. Oakley was sitting at her desk as my mother approached her.

"Good morning, Mrs. Oakley."

"Good morning, Mrs. Peele. What can I do for you?"

My mother looked at her. "It seems that Amy is allergic to the varnish on the desks. I brought a piece of oil cloth that she needs to have on top of her desk so she doesn't break out again. I hope that won't be a problem."

Mrs. Oakley nodded, "Amy, you can keep it on your desk during class time, but when we get ready to leave for the day, you need to put it back inside your desk."

I nodded.

My mother thanked her, and I followed her out to the front of the school to say goodbye. But Sister Mary Jane stopped her before she could open the door to leave.

"Mrs. Peele, can I see you in the office for a moment? There seems to be a problem with your bill."

My mother looked at Sister Mary Jane, and then at me. "Amy, you run outside and play, and don't forget your oil cloth." She followed the Sister into her office and I ran outside to a place where I knew I could see my mother and Sister Mary Jane through one of the school windows. Sister Mary Jane was holding up a book, and pointing to certain parts of the pages. Mom took out her checkbook and wrote a check, and they both seemed to be smiling as my mother departed.

My rash stayed on my hands, and occasionally it popped up inside my elbows when I got really nervous. But once summer rolled around, and I was swimming at the Aqua Center every day, everything looked normal again. Mom credited it to all the chlorine in the pool and the sunshine. I knew that it was the freedom I felt in the water when I swam that caused me to feel calm inside and not itch.

ST. IRENAEUS SCHOOL
1959-60

ST. IRENAEUS SCHOOL
1957-58

Amy

John

5

Public School

"You're not supposed to talk about underwear out loud in public."

—Amy

The summer after my dad left was when we found out we were going to have to go to public schools starting the next fall. Up until then, we had been in Catholic schools our entire lives. According to Mom, they were the only place you could get a good education and discipline all for one price.

Even before Dad left, Mom was working full time as a private-duty nurse. Now her salary had to pay for everything, since my father wasn't even paying child support. All those years of my parents and brothers and sisters bragging about our high-class education came to an abrupt halt. All my eight-year-old brain could think of was no more uniforms, no more mean nuns, and a real playground instead of bare blacktop.

That summer was the same as always, except that we didn't know if we would end up going to Lake Wawasee or not. But our mother delivered on our annual summer vacation, and we headed down Route 30 to see Mogi and Aunt Mary in Syracuse just like always. Mom looked more tired than usual as she pulled the station wagon out of the driveway and began the three-hour trip. We always left early in the morning, so that we could get to the lake in enough time for our first long swim.

Toward the tail end of the vacation that summer, Aunt Mary told Helen and me that she was taking us shopping for school clothes. This was the first time she had ever taken us shopping. She steered her white Cadillac away from the lake, past the Dairy Queen, and out of Syracuse. This was going to be a big trip. Twenty air-conditioned minutes later, she pulled into the driveway of Rinker's. It was fancier and bigger than the five-and-dime on Kale Island, and was two towns away, in Warsaw. As I walked through the door, the smell of brand new was everywhere. As the youngest kids, Helen and I were used to hand-me-downs from Char and Kerry. We rarely got new clothes. I started to look around slowly, not quite believing that Aunt Mary would actually buy us brand new clothes. Rinker's reminded me of the Sears catalog I wished my way through each year. So many things to touch and explore. The manager of Rinker's stopped what he was doing to greet us. I was always impressed with the type of attention Aunt Mary got from all the storeowners, as if she was a movie star or something.

"Good morning, Mrs. Evans. What can I do for you today?"

Aunt Mary looked down at the manager, who was quite a bit shorter than her, and pointed her thin index finger at Helen and me.

"My nieces need some clothes to start the school year. Nothing too fancy," she said in her deep, raspy voice. Before she'd even finished what she was saying, he was walking toward the side of the store filled with children's clothes. As Helen and I started to get distracted by a pile of pretty blouses, I heard Aunt Mary bark, "Give them each a dozen pair of the white underwear, and assorted socks." My sister and I turned red. You weren't supposed to talk about underwear out loud in public. We started to pick out shorts, blouses, and skirts, looking over to Aunt Mary every so often for her approval. "You girls have to wear them. Pick out five outfits, and then let's get back home." Helen and I quickly turned to each other in disbelief. This must be what movie stars felt like. We began to select colorful blouses with matching skirts.

Upon leaving the store, the manager loaded all the packages into the trunk of Aunt Mary's fancy Cadillac. We were so excited to get back to Mogi's house to try everything on and have a fashion show. We felt like Pollyanna when she got all those new clothes.

We had one more stop—at Pelcher's Shoe Store right in downtown Syracuse. We went there every year for the pair of shoes Mogi always bought us that were supposed to last us all school year. Mr. Pelcher always smiled when he saw us coming—six pairs of shoes! "So, where's the rest of the gang?" he asked when Aunt Mary walked in with the two of us trailing behind her.

Aunt Mary sat down in one of his chairs, part of her overflowing on each side. "Oh, they'll be in later. For now, I have these two young ladies." Helen and I beamed as we started to look at our options. Usually our mother would pre-select what our choices would be, but Aunt Mary wasn't moving. There was a pause as Helen and I glanced over at Aunt Mary, who was lighting a Pall Mall cigarette. "Go ahead, pick out a pair of shoes and let's get moving," she said.

"Any pair?" I asked timidly.

"You have to wear them." Helen and I each picked out a pair of black patent leather Mary Janes. We were grinning ear to ear as we walked out of the store with our boxes.

When we got back to Mogi's, we showed her each outfit, and then we carefully folded our clothes and packed them for the ride home. Our brothers and sisters didn't seem to care that we got all these new clothes. As soon as we got home to Park Forest, we rushed into our bedroom, hung up our clothes, and put our shoeboxes on the closet floor.

The night before my first day of school, I laid out my new outfit, took my new shoes out of their box, and put a new pair of socks inside them. I could hardly sleep that night. I fell asleep to the smell of new shoes and the picture of how great I would look and feel, starting my life at a brand new school.

The next morning, Helen and I jumped out of the single bed we shared and put on our outfits. My bright blue and yellow flowered cotton blouse still had its crisp feel as I tucked it into my navy blue skirt. I slipped on matching navy blue ankle socks and my new shoes. I never had anything match like this before. Helen looked as great as I felt. Char had hot oatmeal and toast waiting for us in the kitchen. Mom had left for work an hour earlier. We were very careful not to spill as we rushed through breakfast and then ran down the hall and brushed our teeth.

Charlene stopped us at the front door.

"Amy, you know where Blackhawk School is. You went to kindergarten there. Walk Helen to her class and make sure you two walk home together. Remember, you're in fourth grade now, and Helen is in second."

I nodded my head. We played at the playground at Blackhawk every summer, and I knew what grade I was in.

Helen and I held hands and ran out the door, across the front lawn, and down our cross street, Oswego. We saw other neighborhood kids walking in the same direction. Helen and I were so proud of our new selves and we skipped for at least a block. A new world awaited us, and together we were ready.

Helen and Amy

6

The Letter

"You are a bold and brassy girl!"
—Sister Dorothea to Amy

The first day of school at Blackhawk, the thing that most caught my attention was all the equipment on the playground. It wasn't just a barren blacktop like at St. Irenaeus. All the kids were friendly, and I joined the band and played the clarinet. There was gym class with real equipment. I was happy, and I quickly made a group of fun girlfriends. All of the new things and friends helped me not think about Dad being gone quite as much.

On September twenty-fifth, a couple weeks into my new school, I celebrated my ninth birthday, my first birthday without Dad. I wondered if the ritual would still be the same. At our house you got to pick your favorite dinner, which was fried chicken, mashed potatoes, and corn for me. You also didn't have to do any household chores for the whole day. When Mom got home from her seven-to-three shift at St. James Hospital, she quickly changed her clothes and called out to me.

"Amy, get in the car and we'll go get your birthday present."

I didn't hesitate and hopped into the car right away, feeling proud to be nine years old. We drove into Chicago Heights, the next town over from Park Forest, where she pulled into the S&H green stamp store. I rushed out of the car and into the store to view all the cool toys and dolls set up right next to the household appliances. The lady at the counter looked through her blue plastic eyeglasses.

"How many books do you have?"

My mom pulled a stack of green stamps from her purse and answered, "We have five full books, and it's my daughter's birthday today. Can you show her what shelf she can pick from?"

The lady pointed to a nearby shelf and I quickly began to inventory every single thing. I came to a screeching halt when I saw a doll with two separate outfits in her box.

"I want the doll."

"Are you sure?" my mother asked.

"Yes, I want the doll. Look at her beautiful outfits."

I could tell my mother was not pleased with my selection, but she put the green stamps on the counter and the lady reached up for the box with the doll and her outfits and handed it to me. I don't remember even walking out to the car.

As we drove home, my mother turned to me and said, "This is your last doll, Amy. You're getting too old for dolls."

I didn't care what she said. I had the doll, and I couldn't wait to show her to Helen. When I got home, I played with the doll, changing her clothes over and over. My dinner plate was heaped with a huge mountain of mashed potatoes with butter dripping down the sides, two pieces of fried chicken— my favorite, the dark meat—and a pile of golden yellow corn with butter, salt, and pepper. Every bite tasted better than the last one. Charlene had made my birthday cake, vanilla cake with chocolate frosting, and each of us polished off our pieces with ice cream on top. Dessert was never an option during weekday dinners, and only occasionally on the weekends. Any time we asked for dessert, my mother's standard response would be, "Desert the table!"

For the next two years, I couldn't have been happier. I had my first crushes on Wiley Christopher and Bill Cory. I made lots of new friends. In fifth grade, my favorite teacher, Mrs. Perryman, let me keep a shoebox—a home for my two troll dolls—inside my desk. The dolls smelled like sweet plastic, and I had made their clothes. It was my own little family at school.

The summer after fifth grade, we took our usual summer trip to Lake Wawasee. When we got home, a couple of weeks before I was to start sixth grade, my mother dropped the bomb.

She called everyone into the kitchen after dinner and told us to sit at the picnic table for one of her family meetings. We were brown and healthy from a summer of swimming and playing outside.

She looked at Helen and me.

"I've made a deal with the nuns at St. Irenaeus, and they have agreed to let you two come back to finish off your elementary education. Aunt Mary and Mogi will help me with the tuition. Aunt Mary will continue to pay for Char and Kerry to go to Sacred Heart, and Bob and John will stay at Marion. You know how important it is to me to have all six of you in Catholic schools."

My heart sank. I had new friends, had learned how to play the clarinet, and the teachers were human. I was so mad, but knew better than to say anything for fear of getting my face slapped and having Mom ask who I thought I was.

Helen and I walked to St. Irenaeus the first day of school in our crisply starched white blouses and red plaid skirts. Our white socks and black and white saddle shoes reluctantly drew us closer. I had Sister Dorothea. She was ugly, fat, and short, and wore the standard black nun glasses. She yelled at me repeatedly the first day.

"Miss Peele, we do not allow talking here. I don't know what you learned at those public schools, but I demand quiet in this class. Please write each of your spelling words ten times." By the end of the day, I was writing each spelling word one hundred times.

When I got home, Mom was so excited to hear about my first day back at St. Irenaeus that I just pretended a smile and shook my head. She assumed I was happy to be back.

I was miserable, though, and by the second week it was unbearable. At recess that Wednesday, I left the school playground and walked over to Blackhawk, and into the principal's office.

"I'd like to enroll myself in school here," I told Mr. Windhelm. I looked into his eyes, expecting him to say yes and direct me to my sixth grade classroom.

"Does your mother know that you're here?"

I frowned at him. "No."

"Your mother needs to enroll you here, Amy," he told me. "You can't do that yourself. You need to go back to St. Irenaeus. I'll ask Mrs. Beckman to drive you back."

I stood there not knowing what to do. I really thought

I was out of that prison. I followed Mrs. Beckman to her car and allowed her to drop me off. I was immediately ushered to the office of the principal, Sister Mary Jane. She asked me to sit down in the chair across from her. She sat behind her desk.

"Miss Peele, where have you been? You should know better than to leave school grounds without permission."

"I went to enroll myself back in school at Blackhawk."

She glared at me through her nun glasses. "And just what does Blackhawk have that St. Irenaeus doesn't?"

I knew the answer, but I hesitated. It was a true answer, but I might get in trouble if I told the truth.

"Miss Peele, what is so very special about that public school?"

"Well, they have a lot of things that you don't have."

"Such as?"

She leaned forward, but there was nothing in her hands to hit me with.

"Well, they have a band, and equipment on their playground, and they have gym classes."

Sister Mary Jane stared at me with her thick bushy black eyebrows that hit the white part of her habit. "Anything else?"

"I don't have to wear a uniform."

She stood up and walked around her desk, towering over me with her red face. "I'm calling your mother at work. Go back to class now." I looked up and saw black nose hairs in her flaring nostrils.

I was dead.

I opened the door to Sister Dorothea's class and the whole class looked in my direction. I walked quickly over to my seat. The classroom door opened and sister Mary Jane motioned for Sister Dorothea to come to the door. Sister Dorothea waddled over and stepped outside into the hall. Moments later she stepped back into the classroom.

"Silence! Who do you think you are?! Miss Peele, get up here."

I walked to the front of the classroom and waited for her to slide all of her black material and rosary beads into the proper place.

"You are a bold and brassy girl! Shame on you!"

I could feel my face getting red as she pointed her crooked right index finger at my face. The more she pointed at me, the dizzier I got.

"Go back to your seat. The nerve."

I met Helen after school and walked home as slowly as I could. At home I changed into my play clothes and started in on my homework. I had to write twenty spelling words two hundred times each.

The front screen door slammed and I heard my mother walk into the kitchen and then down the hall. She stopped in front of the bedroom.

"Amy, get in my room. Now."

I followed her into her bedroom.

"Close the door."

She sat on the edge of her double bed. "I work seven days a week, no time off, borrow money to keep you in a Catholic school, and this is the thanks I get! Take your pants down and bend over."

She took Dad's long black leather belt, folded it in half, and snapped it a few times.

"What are you getting this beating for?"

I was already crying. I didn't answer her.

"What are you getting this beating for?!"

She snapped the black double belt again.

"Because I left school." I was shaking.

My mother held the belt in her hand and hauled off and slapped the doubled leather on my bare butt. I yelled out in pain, and kept crying. She hit me several more times, and then stopped.

"Pull up your pants, and stand up."

Tears ran down my face, and my nose was running all over. I hated her, and I hated St. Irenaeus.

"I want you to write Sister Mary Jane a letter, and tell her how much you love her school, and apologize for being so rude and insensitive."

Back in my room, I sat on the edge of my bed, angrier about having to write a letter full of lies than I was about the beating. I wrote the letter I was told to write, showed it to my mother, and gave it to Sister Mary Jane the next day.

Sister just gave me a fake nun smile and thanked me. I hated her. That Friday when I went to confession with the rest of the class, I told Father Reading about the letter and confessed that I was forced to write a pack of lies. I told him maybe my mother should have to say the five Hail Marys and four Our Fathers instead of me but he didn't agree.

I stopped talking to everyone at school for the next three years. I became the most miserable, unpopular kid and I didn't care. All I saw when I looked in the mirror was an ugly girl with long, scraggly brown hair, sad eyes hidden by black plastic glasses, and pimples.

By the end of eighth grade, I realized what a nerd I'd become, and so I decided to use my babysitting money to send myself to Sears Charm School. I learned some make-up skills and how to stand up straight and pirouette. The class ended with a fashion show that I didn't invite anyone to, and I modeled my school uniform.

During the summer between eighth grade and high school, I went swimming at the Aqua Center every day after my chores were done. Each evening, after the pools closed, Tim Cunningham from my eighth grade class walked me home. We innocently taught each other how to make out, and it was fun. He was going to Marion Catholic High School, too.

The day I was supposed to start at Marion, my mother made a last-minute decision to send me to our local public high school, Rich East, instead. The private Catholic girls' high school hadn't kept Charlene and Kerry out of trouble, so she'd decided, why waste any more of Aunt Mary's money?

I showed up on my first day of public high school with some charm, new clothes from Sears, and as an experienced kisser.

SUMMER 1962
WORK LIST - 335 INDIANWOOD
- NO AQUACENTER UNLESS
CHORES ARE DONE !!
BOB (15) - CLEAN BEDROOM - PUT LAUNDRY
   AWAY - WORK @ DANDY'S - 6 P.M.
CHARLENE (13) - FOLD LAUNDRY WHEN
   DONE - KITCHEN CLEAN-UP - BEDROOM
   THEATER - WORK - 1 P.M.
KERRY (12) PUT FOLDED LAUNDRY
   AWAY - CLEAN BEDROOM - HELP KITCHEN
JOHN (10) WALK THE DOGS - PUT
   BIKE AND TOYS AWAY - BEDROOM
   PICK UP YARD TRASH.
AMY (8) HELP WITH LAUNDRY -
   KITCHEN - BEDROOM
HELEN (6) - BEDROOM - HELP
   CHARLENE IF NEEDED
CHARLENE - CHECK CHORES,
   I'LL BE HOME AFTER WORK - 4 P.M
   SEE YOU AT DINNER TIME . LOVE YOU
   HOSP. # - 756-1000 .   MOM

Mom's Daily List

7

Ollie

"Get your white asses out the bed."
—Ollie

From the time I was eight, I woke up to a list of chores written by my mother at six in the morning before she left for her private-duty nursing job at the hospital. Seven days a week, the list was posted on a clipboard, her handwriting always beautiful, a product of her Catholic school education. The list always started with "Good Morning" at the top. She wrote our names in the order of our birth, followed by the chores we were responsible for. Each room of our three-bedroom tract house had to be thoroughly cleaned and checked on the weekends before anyone was permitted to step outside and play.

Usually Charlene was the checker. Her job was to make sure the work was done properly. The chrome in the bathroom needed to be polished, and the entire toilet, inside and out, had to be spotless. No dust, no dirt, no stains, or you start over again. My mother was raised by her Irish grandmother, and our house had to be immaculately clean. It was our job to see this was done.

One Saturday morning when I was ten, I was awakend by the front door slamming shut. There was a fall chill in the air, and before I even opened my eyes I heard a voice that reverberated throughout the house.

"Get your white assess out of bed! Your mother has been up for hours working hard! Go on, get up!"

It was our mechanic, Ollie, who worked at O'Brien's service station. I moved sluggishly under my warm covers in the bottom bunk, my little sister Helen not budging on the top. Since our car was always in the shop, Ollie became an extended family member. He always wore his grey pressed mechanics shirt with his name embroidered over the pocket. He walked back and forth in our hallway, waiting for us to put our feet on the floor before leaving. He knew that if we weren't out of bed we would all go back to sleep as soon as he left. I sat up in bed and he gave me one of his big smiles as he passed by my bedroom door, his black skin contrasting with his white teeth—and the one gold-coated front tooth. He went into my brothers' room and started to holler, "Get your lazy asses up. I have to tow your Buick down to the garage, the transmission isn't working and Mr. O'Brien asked me to come get it. Your mother needs to have a car that works."

Bob immediately got up and made his way to the bathroom, but Ollie stopped him in the hall right in front of our bedroom. Bob had recently turned sixteen and passed his drivers test.

"This is the second transmission your car has gone through in three months. You have any ideas how that could be?"

"Beats me, maybe the transmissions are bad," he said, scratching himself the way boys do in the mornings.

"No, they were brand new. Took them out of the box myself. Your mom said she hasn't taken any long trips; just back and forth to the hospital and to the Forest Preserves several times. She said you took the car for a date on Sunday. Go anywhere that was really hilly?"

"Nope, just to the dunes for the day."

"The ones in Indiana? Don't you have to drive by US 30 drag strip to get there?"

"I think that's near there. Not really sure. When do you think you can have the car done? I have to pick Mom up at four."

"You bring your little sisters by the garage when you walk down to the station. I told her I would watch them tonight. She's taking you older ones to the Parents Without Partners meeting in Crete."

"That's the first I heard about it. But okay. I'll come by around 3:30," Bob grumbled.

Ollie stepped into our bedroom, "You two little ones are coming to my place tonight for a barbeque. Get your chores done and I'll see you later."

Ollie headed back down the hall and shouted to Bob again, "Bob, you need to change all four tires when you drag race, not just the back ones." I heard Bob go back into his room, where John was still sleeping, and shut the door behind him. Ollie went out the front door and I heard his loud pickup truck drive away.

One by one, we girls got up and shuffled off to the kitchen for One-Eyed Petes. We'd seen them made on TV. Charlene, now fifteen, did most of the grocery shopping and cooking for the family. "Who wants a Pete?" she asked, and Kerry, Helen and I were quick to respond in the affirmative.

As Charlene spread the butter into the pan, Helen took the top off the cinnamon bottle and used it to punch out perfect holes in each piece of soft white bread, which she'd laid out neatly on the kitchen counter. I stood next to her and buttered one side of the bread and its companion circle.

Charlene looked at us and began in with her instructional lesson. "Now you have to get the butter nice and hot in the pan. Not burnt brown, but hot. Hand me the bread, Helen."

Char put three pieces of bread in the pan and I could hear the sizzle and the smell of butter bubbling. She took one egg at a time and cracked them neatly in the middle of the bread where the holes were. Then she turned the whole thing over so that the other side of the bread got crunchy, too.

"Kerry, you get the frozen orange juice out and make a pitcher." Kerry didn't sass back for a change and went about making the orange juice, smashing the frozen lumps of it against the side of the plastic pitcher with a wooden spoon. I stood over the heating duct so that my nightgown billowed out in the blowing hot air. I did this every morning once winter came. It was warm and comforting.

Char declared the final task, "Amy, you get the paper plates out and use the wicker holders and set the table."

The four of us sat at the picnic table where we ate our meals and had family meetings.

I salted my One-Eyed Pete and began to cut it up into small pieces so that the crunchy, buttery bread could absorb the loose egg yolk in the middle. I took my first bite, which was a combination of crunchy bread, warm egg yolk, and a bit of salt.

Bob and John entered the kitchen and immediately protested, "Hey, where's our grub?"

Char didn't even look up. "Make it yourself."

Bob looked at John and said, "You get the bread."

Bob turned the stove on and gave Charlene a disdainful look. They usually didn't start fighting this early. John took out four pieces of bread at the point when Char stood up to clear her plate. "John, you know we're only allowed one each. Put back the other two pieces. We have to make this loaf last through lunch."

Bob sneered as the butter he put in the pan began to bubble, but didn't say a thing. He knew the rules.

After John had finished holing the bread, he headed into the living room to turn on the television. "Hey, why won't this thing work?" John loved to watch it so much we called him "TV Eyes."

He tapped the side of the brown wooden box as he looked around the back to see if the cord was plugged in. It was. From the kitchen, Char said, "Mom took a few of the TV tubes with her to work, so no TV today. Enjoy your breakfast."

After our chores had been checked by Char, Helen and I went out to play until Bob yelled for us to get ready to go. We followed him down Indianwood for three long blocks until we got to the front office of O'Brien's Phillips 66 service station.

"Hello there," Mr. O'Brien welcomed us, peering over his glasses, his thick black eyebrows and mustache twitching back and forth.

Bob moved toward the counter, "Ollie said to come by to pick up the car." Mr. O'Brien put his hand around Bob's shoulder and motioned for us to sit down. He then guided Bob into the garage where the cars were hoisted in the air with men working under them. Mr. O'Brien and Bob walked over to Ollie as he wiped the grease off his hands.

"Look, Helen, I think they're yelling at Bob," I said, standing so I could get a better view. Bob's face turned red and we watched Ollie pointing at our car and then at Bob. When I saw them coming back toward us, I quickly sat down.

"Here's a nickel for both you girls," Mr. O'Brien said. "Go over to Kresge's and get yourself some candy and come right back. Ollie should be ready to leave by then." He took a handful of change from his dirty work pants pockets and held out some coins. We each selected a nickel. "Thank you, Mr. O'Brien," we said in unison.

We raced across the long parking lot, past Marshall Fields, past Branson's, the fancy ladies clothes store, and straight into Kresge's, slowing down only when we approached the candy aisle. Kresge's had everything any five and dime store should, and an assortment of items made and sold cheaply. I felt comfortable there, not like at Marshall Fields where I always felt I was too poor to even walk around. I lived in constant fear that someone would ask me if I had enough money to even be looking at those fancy Barbie doll clothes.

There was penny candy and higher-priced candy on the Kresge's shelves. There wasn't much time to make the important choice. Should I buy one big nickel item, like a Turkish Taffy or Heath Bar that would take some time to eat, or five pieces of assorted candy? While I was mulling over my choices, Helen had made her selection and was already at the cash register. I grabbed a vanilla Turkish Taffy and met her up at the front. As we headed back to the garage, Helen started to pop a Good & Plenty into her mouth and I bit off a piece of the white smooth taffy, chewing it slowly. The rich creamy flavor of vanilla filled my mouth and the thick taffy teased all the silver filings my dentist, Dr. Hammer, had so carefully placed in my teeth. We walked slowly so we'd finish our treats before we saw anyone who'd dare use the word "share" in a sentence with regard to our candy.

Ollie was writing some numbers on a piece of paper when we walked into the garage. He handed it to Mr. O'Brien and said, "Here's the total for the parts. Don't charge her for my labor. She don't have enough money for groceries for those kids."

Bob backed our car out of the garage, honking and waving at us.

Mr. O'Brien opened up the register, lifted up the cash tray, and slipped the paper under it. "Just tell their mom to pay what she can, when she can, a little every month, good faith money, Ollie. You know what I mean." Mr. O'Brien looked over at Helen and me, "You girls going over to Ollie's for the best barbeque in town?" We both nodded our heads as we munched on the last bites of sugar.

"Come on now, get in the truck," Ollie said. "We need to get home, my neighbors are waiting on me."

We headed out of lily-white Park Forest, down highway 30, and toward Chicago Heights, which was a dense collection of apartment buildings with a few houses sprinkled in between. Ollie made a stop at a liquor store that had bars over the windows and came out with a six-pack of Schlitz malt liquor and a carton of Lucky Strikes. He drove into the alley behind his apartment building and parked in front of his garage.

"You girls come on up while I take a shower, and then you can help me cook." We headed up the back stairs into a sparsely furnished kitchen and living room.

"Sit down on the couch and watch some TV, I'll be right out." The house smelled like the oil from the garage. Ollie turned on the tube and *Leave to Beaver* came on, one of my favorites. Before I knew it, Ollie was behind us smelling clean. "Come on girls, let's go do some barbequeing."

We followed him back down the stairs and into the garage where there was a huge fifty-gallon drum sliced in half, with a metal grill balanced on top of one half. Ollie set about cleaning the old coals out of it and replacing them with new ones. "I'll be needing a lot of these today. It's the first Saturday night of the month and it's my turn to que for the whole neighborhood. You girls just relax and enjoy yourselves, let me know if you need anything. Don't go wandering off."

He flipped the switch on the old broken-down radio that was plugged into the wall and out came sound. "You young'uns listen up now, that's Ella Fitzgerald, the first lady of song." I didn't know what that meant, but the sound of her creamy voice filled the air. I felt as safe in Ollie's garage as I did in the waters of Lake Wawasee. The sound of music pulled neighbors toward the garage carrying bowls filled with potato salad, coleslaw, and six-packs of Schlitz malt liquor. One large man brought a blue velvet bag with a fancy bottle in it and put it on the shelf alongside two small glasses.

"You ready for a little, Quil?" he asked, motioning his head toward Ollie. I'd never heard anyone call him Quil before.

Ollie nodded his head, "Let me go up and get the chicken out of the fridge and I'll be right down."

The garage had filled with black men and women who looked about the same age as Ollie. They had kids close to our age who started to dance and we joined in. It felt like

I had swallowed the music and my body knew just what to do with it. The adults didn't pay us any attention, just an occasional chuckle our way. The smell of the chicken sizzling on the grill seemed to increase the energy of everybody in the garage. The ladies and men were smoking Lucky Strikes, sipping their beer, and laughing.

A long black car slowly drove by the alley and stopped in front of the open garage. Ollie's smile went away and he squinted his eyes, "You go on now, there's nothing here for you, go on." The car didn't move, though, and everyone stopped and stared at the rough-looking fellas. They were staring at Helen and me. We stopped dancing and moved toward the back of the garage.

One of them poked his head out the passenger window. "You cooking white meat tonight, Quil? Mind if we join you?"

Ollie put down his beer and walked toward the car with a few other men, but before they got there the car sped away. The music went louder and the buzz of all the rich voices returned the garage back to its rhythm. Big platters of chicken were put on card tables that Ollie and his lady friend had set up. People spooned heaping scoops of rich potato salad and coleslaw onto one side of their plates. On the other side they laid down a piece of Wonder Bread and placed the sauce-drenched chicken on top. I had never seen chicken served that way. One of the big ladies handed Helen and me each a plate and we sat on the garage floor with the rest of the kids. My first bite of sweet warm sauce and moist chicken meat was the most scrumptious combination of flavors I had ever experienced. I was one with the chicken, eating every last bit of meat down to the bone and licking my fingers so as not to miss a drop of sauce.

The big lady looked down and laughed, "There's plenty more, honey, you go getchya a piece now. Quil, you feed these poor girls, they need to put some fat on their bones."

Ollie looked up, smiled, and waved for me to come over to him and he put more chicken on my spotless plate, "Go on now, get, and send your little sister on over here before she starts feeling sorry for herself she didn't get as much as you."

Helen was already marching past me to Ollie with her empty white paper plate, big blue eyes shining.

There was a comforting hum as everyone sat in Ollie's garage and ate. There wasn't much conversation except for an occasional, "Damn Good, Quil, damn good." As the pile of paper plates started to fill the garbage can, the pace of the music got faster.

One tall man yelled across the garage, "That Sam Cooke, Quil?" Ollie just smiled.

The pretty bottles came out of the velvet blue bags and a strong smell of liquor filled the air as conversations got louder and louder. Big fat ladies danced with each other and one of them grabbed my arm to get up and dance. Not wanting to be rude, I stood up and moved my hips back and forth, feeling awkward as the other kids stood up and started to really shake it. One of the big ladies bent down and whispered in my ear, "Just close your eyes darling and feel the music. Let it get into your body. Ain't no one cares what you look like, just feel it."

I closed my eyes and felt the rhythm and moved my body around, keeping my feet still. Then all of sudden I smelled her close to my ear, "It's okay to move those feet, honey. They're part of you, too."

I watched the other kids move, saw the smile in their eyes. They were part of the music. Slowly, I imitated them, getting into the flow and not seeing anyone in the garage, just feeling the beat. I don't remember when Helen joined in, but she got into the flow, too. I occasionally glanced around to find Ollie, who was never far away. He would flash a big smile, gold tooth sparkling, which told me everything was alright. The evening ended when I heard four dreaded words, "It's time to go," from him.

About half the people had already left, a few at a time, but the garage still felt full with the dancing and laughter of those that remained. Ollie filled up a plastic glass with some liquor and motioned Helen and me into his truck. He drove us home in silence, sipping his whiskey and smoking his cigarettes with some jazz music playing on the radio. We passed the car that had driven by the garage earlier. Ollie didn't pay any attention, even though they yelled something at us. I caught the word *white,* but Ollie didn't say a word.

It was late when Helen and I slid out of the front seat of the truck. Ollie opened the front door to our house. "Now go on and get ready for bed and don't give your Mama no lip," he told us. Mom was sitting at the kitchen table doing paperwork and we hugged her hello.

"You girls have a good time tonight with Ollie?" We nodded, and I looked over at him. "Ollie, how come all your friends call you Quil, and we call you Ollie?" I asked.

He picked me up and smiled, "It's my last name, Quilla, Oliver Quilla. It's my nickname. Do you have a nickname?"

I looked over at Mom, "Do I, Mom?"

"No sweetheart, not yet, but your friends will give you one someday. Now you girls go brush your teeth and get to bed. You have church in the morning, and I have to work."

"Again?" Helen and I asked at the same time.

"You work every day of the week, Mom." I said.

"Someone has to pay these bills and put food on the table. It's time for bed. Say goodnight."

I gave Ollie a big hug and whispered into his ear, "Thanks for the delicious barbeque, Quil." He chuckled.

Mom gave Helen and me a kiss. "If you stop by the garage after church and show him the church bulletin to prove you went, maybe Ollie will give you some candy money."

"Only if they're in bed by the time I count to twenty. One, two."

Helen and I ran down the hall and grabbed our

toothbrushes for a lightning-fast brush. We went pee and threw our pajamas on. We heard Ollie's voice by the front door, "Nineteen." I threw the blanket over me as I lay down in the lower bunk.

"Twenty." I smiled. Nothing motivated us like candy.

I heard my mom say to Ollie, "What do I owe for the transmission? I'll have to pay Mr. O'Brien in a month. The next paycheck goes to the mortgage."

"Bobby is gonna work it off. He offered and Mr. O'Brien is holding him to it. Don't worry about this one." Their voices trailed off and I fell asleep and dreamt that I was in a dance contest in Ollie's garage, and everyone was dancing and clapping and cheering me along.

Danny and Bubs

8

Judges of the Round Table

"Children should be seen and not heard."
—Aunt Mary

Cocktail hour was a serious time around Aunt Mary's house. She had a clock hanging on her wall that had only number fives. Every day the usual adults would start gravitating toward Aunt Mary's remodeled garage at five on the dot. Aunt Mary did not like anyone in her home, so she entertained in her garage.

We knew when it was getting close to five because Bubs and Danny would pull up in their loud white pickup truck. They only lived about a block away, but I never saw them walk over. Bubs was just under five feet, had a round belly, a chubby nose and cheeks, and skinny legs. Her hair was short, dirty blonde, and curled close to her head. She always had a lit cigarette hanging from one side of her mouth, or on its way to it. She looked straight through Helen and me, as if we were invisible.

Danny was about six-foot-two, and had black hair and a mustache. He looked a little like Clark Gable from far away. He had a broad strong chest and a small beer belly, and was nicer and softer than Bubs. Aunt Mary was usually stationed in her chair, reading the paper and smoking a cigarette, when they'd enter the garage without knocking. The back screen door opened onto the yard. It was always open and there was a good cross breeze.

The year I was nine and Helen was six, Mogi moved out of her white house and across the island when she married her new husband, Grandpa Carl. Gogi had died a few years earlier, and none of us liked this change of events because it meant we had to get a ride to Aunt Mary's and Kale Beach, or walk the five miles rather than having the quick five-minute run down to the lake. But that summer Helen and I still spent a lot of time in Aunt Mary's yard, blowing the feather wisps off the flowers and making dandelion jewelry. When cocktail hour was getting near, we liked to sit close enough to the door so we could see the adults and overhear their conversation without being noticed.

With a deep, raspy voice, Danny said, "Hi Mary, can I fix you a drink?" Without waiting for a response, we heard him head over to the liquor cabinet, take out some glasses, and walk over to the freezer for ice.

"It's about that time, isn't it?" Aunt Mary said. I could imagine exactly the way she looked, responding without even looking up from her paper.

Bubs waddled over to an empty chair at the big round table, sat down, and lit a cigarette. The tone of their voices was low and steady. This was the warm-up.

Danny poured three glasses of Pinch Scotch and placed one in front of each of the ladies. He pulled his chair up to the table and took a drink. Cocktail hour had officially begun.

Danny never got to sit very long because Aunt Mary always had a list of chores for him to do between drinks, either in the house or the garage. The three of them could sit there for the longest time without talking, comfortable with their joint silence.

Helen and I heard the sound of gravel under car wheels and looked around to see Mogi and Grandpa Carl. They got out of their car carrying bags of groceries. We waved but left them alone, knowing better than to bother them during cocktail hour.

Danny stood up as they walked in. "Get you two a drink?"

Mogi replied, "I'll have my usual." She sat next to Aunt Mary, but there wasn't any exchange of affection. Grandpa Carl was standing in front of a large blue map tacked to the garage wall that outlined all the good fishing spots on Lake Wawasee. He had placed at least half of the pushpins in it himself. He turned around and looked at Danny. "I'll have a shot of Jack and a cold beer. Mary, I found a good spot right near the root beer stand. Caught four bass there early this morning. Brought them to fry up tonight. Lillian, would you soak them in milk?" Mogi got up and headed for the sink.

Aunt Mary finally lowered her paper, signaled for Danny to refill her drink, and looked at Grandpa Carl. "Thank God you brought some food for all those kids— they're eating us out of house and home. We'll send them down to the Dairy Queen after dinner, so we can get a game of cards going." Aunt Mary put a cigarette to her mouth as Danny bent over and lit it for her.

Helen and I could never understand why Bubs and Danny always waited on Aunt Mary the way they did. I once overheard my mother tell my father that Bubs was the Madam and Danny the bouncer in Aunt Mary's whorehouse during the Depression. Which was why Aunt Mary was so rich, because she made so much money back then. This was a subject we could never broach with Aunt Mary, so there was no way to confirm or deny.

I often got lost in thought seeing our elders sitting around the table every night for cocktail hour. They insisted on being treated as important and wise, even though I knew they were not. It was as though they were the ultimate judges, regardless of whether they were smart or sober or drunk. Thick cigarette smoke hovered over the table, and the sound of ice cubes clinking against glasses provided a dull background for the loud conversations that escalated by the hour. By the time Mom joined the crowd, my siblings and I made sure to quietly disappear until someone yelled for dinnertime. Aunt Mary's hard glances told us that children should be seen and not heard.

When it was time for dinner, and for us to join the group at the table, Mogi brought plates of sliced, homegrown tomatoes, fried fish, coleslaw, and a stack of white bread to the big wooden table. After a fast paced "Blessed our Lord and these our gifts," we devoured the food.

After dinner, it was Charlene and Kerry's turn to do the dishes. Mogi turned to Helen and me and handed us two leftover chunks of bread.

"You girls go down to the Chinese gardens and feed the swans. This bread won't be any good by tomorrow morning. Be careful not to fall in."

Helen and I skipped down to the most magical place on Kale Island. It was only minutes from Aunt Mary's house, and being there felt like entering another world. A man we didn't know owned the piece of property with a lagoon on it. In tribute to his Asian wife, he'd built a bright red pagoda and bridge in the middle of the lagoon. We knew we weren't supposed to be there—that it was intended for their family only. He and his wife would go out there for lunch or afternoon tea. The lagoon was long and wide, and had real dogfish that barked. It was against the law to fish in it, especially to catch the dogfish, but that didn't stop Bob and John from bringing a couple home in a bucket once. We didn't eat them, though, and Mogi made them take them back.

When Helen and I got there, a family of white swans was gracefully swimming around the lagoon. We tore up the bread into tiny pieces and tossed them into the lagoon. We made the feeding last a long time. We stood there long after we ran out of bread, in our summer shorts and tops, peacefully traveling into our own private imaginations. I wonder if Mogi ever knew the simple peace that summer errand brought Helen and me.

As the sun set over the pagoda, we raced back to Aunt Mary's and then headed down to the Dairy Queen by foot, which was a two-mile walk one way. I think the adults wanted us out of their hair and knew it would take us a long time if we walked. Bob led the way, waving a five-dollar bill in the air. As we walked by the neighboring cottages with twinkling lights peeking through each window, the humidity of the day was wearing off and a small cool breeze provided some relief. Fireflies gently lit our pathway.

By the time we wandered home, with bellies full of Dilly Bars and ice cream sundaes, the judges were wandering in the direction of their cars. I marveled at the sense of righteousness they seemed to possess. All of them except for Mogi seemed to look down their noses at us like we were beggars. I always tried to stay away from them and their opinions, how perfect could they really be anyway? Just because they were the adults didn't make them God.

Mogi always drove Grandpa Carl home, as she never had more than two drinks. It didn't matter whether Danny or Bubs had too much to drink since their drive home was only a block. Aunt Mary was nestled in her small yellow house. Her lights were still on, but the invisible "Don't bother me" sign was flashing. The evening court had been adjourned, and the judges had retreated to their respective homes. Who knew what person or persons they passed sentence on that night, convinced in their drunken stupors that they had once again solved all the problems of Kale Island, and that Kale Island was lucky to have such high-powered, intelligent adults to make it a safer and better place.

Noggie and Aunt Mary

9

The Noggie Prodder

"Not even we could get Aunt Mary to move like that."
—Amy

A unt Mary had a love for boxers, and a strong belief that dogs and children should be well disciplined. She had several boxers over the years, and when one died, she'd buy another one and give him the same name: Noggie. I met the first Noggie the summer I was eight. I watched him as he pranced in and out of Aunt Mary's house and garage. The first time I saw him, he had white bandages on his tail and ears. When Aunt Mary saw us eyeing the addition to her family, she snarled, "I had his ears and tail clipped, so don't touch them or he'll bite you." We weren't sure why she'd done this. We would have never cut Buckshot and Rebel's tails. Regardless, we were thrilled she had gotten a dog. Maybe if Aunt Mary started to like dogs, she'd start to like children, too.

The afternoon we arrived at the lake that year, Aunt Mary encouraged us to run off to get our first dip in Lake Wawasee. We sprinted barefoot down the road. I was so excited to be there that my feet barely touched the ground as I ran. We jumped in and swam as fast as we could to the white raft that floated a half-mile out and started our long morning of King of the Raft. Dodging big black horse flies, we swam all morning, not paying any mind to the time until our stomachs started growling for lunch.

I am sure it had to be a scary sight for Mogi to see six hungry, wet kids heading toward her house all at once. Mogi anticipated this deluge, though, and she always had prepared sandwiches on wonderful soft white bread that was unique to her house. The filling of the sandwich was usually some combination of cold meat and cheese with mayonnaise and fat slices of homegrown tomatoes. Her sandwiches always tasted better than the ones we had at home. Mogi made grape Kool-Aid with the full amount of sugar, unlike at home where Mom only used half. We sat outside and happily ate while Mogi kept a stern but loving eye on us. If you looked up fast enough, sometimes you could see her smiling.

After we cleaned up, it was time for an afternoon nap.

Mogi sprinkled us throughout the various rooms of the house and we tried to fall asleep. But we were all so excited to begin our summer vacation that it was hard to still our minds. Other than the Fourth of July parade and fireworks in Central Park back in Park Forest, our two weeks at Lake Wawasee were the highlight of every summer. As I lay down next to Helen, we started to plan how we would get our first stash of penny candy money. Mogi quickly put a silence to our conversation, though, threatening no more swimming if we didn't take a nap right then.

It's hard to say if it was one or two hours later, or who had actually fallen asleep, but one by one we got up. The voices coming from Aunt Mary's garage drew us toward it. We didn't want to miss out on any big plans for the summer. We entered the garage to find Aunt Mary and Mogi sitting at the big round table smoking their cigarettes and discussing dinner plans. Lying on top of the table next to Aunt Mary was what appeared to be a metal pipe, about six inches long. We knew better than to ask what it was because the automatic answer would be, "It's none of your god damn business." We'd find out later that it was an electric cattle prod used to move cattle quickly through the slaughter lines, but for now we were about to get a demonstration of how it worked.

When Noggie saw me come in, he immediately stood, ran to me, and jumped up. Aunt Mary yelled for him to stop and come back and sit next to her, but Noggie ignored her. Aunt Mary stood up, grabbed the cattle prod, and headed over toward Noggie and me. He turned his head, looked over his wagging stubbed tail, and started running around the table away from her. But Aunt Mary was on a mission. I just stood and stared as this six-foot, large-assed woman chased her little boxer around her table. Not even we kids could get Aunt Mary to move like that. She doubled back and caught Noggie right in the butt with the prodder. There was a short buzzing sound and a yelp from Noggie. Aunt Mary belted out a raspy "SIT" and Noggie complied immediately.

I looked at my silent, open-mouthed siblings. As Noggie took his place next to Aunt Mary, she glanced up and scanned her audience. She picked up the instrument of torture and said, "This is a Noggie Prodder and it gives Noggie a little jolt of electricity to let him know who the boss is. He is a young dog and he needs to learn to obey, just like you kids. Don't think I won't use it on you if I hear any back talk. Now get outside and play. It's a beautiful day, and close that screen door tight."

We immediately bolted for the screen door, grabbed our towels off the clothesline, and raced back down to the lake. What we never saw was the look exchanged between Aunt Mary and Mogi. I'm sure they waited until we were out of earshot before getting a good belly laugh from the looks on our faces. I never did get zapped with the Noggie Prodder, even though my brother John claims he got it once. Come to think of it, I rarely saw Aunt Mary use it on Noggie, but I imagine Noggie was a quick learner.

Aunt Mary

10

Fishing

"You catch it, you clean it, you eat it."
—Aunt Mary

When Carl Nickel, Mogi's husband after Gogi, came into our lives, fishing on a pontoon became a more standard part of our summer vacations. He was a tall man with a big belly, a full head of waving gray hair, and false teeth. He loved to be on the water, but never in the water. Grandpa Carl won us over when he took us two at a time across Lake Wawasee in his small motorboat and bought us ice cream. That was all it took—ice cream and the fact that he didn't try to throw us overboard.

When Mogi moved in with Grandpa Carl, she claimed it was going to be a short-term thing because the house he lived in—a small pink three-bedroom house on the other side of Syracuse—was the house that he and his first wife lived in. She told him he needed to build them a new house to start their new life together. I thought that was a little crazy since they were both already well into their fifties, but Grandpa Carl did build Mogi a new house—even further away from Aunt Mary's.

I don't remember Mom ever talking about any wedding, but the following summer we went to Grandpa Carl's house on a different part of Lake Wawasee. The year after that, Grandpa Carl built Mogi their new house and so we went to yet another house, which was right on a channel that fed into the lake. There was an upstairs and a downstairs that faced the water with a screened-in porch. We saw much less of Aunt Mary that summer, and I imagine she must have been relieved not to see all of us tromping toward her house.

Fishing was a way of life at Lake Wawasee. Why else would anyone live by a great big natural lake? As a child I would listen to the fishermen stop by Aunt Mary's garage and tell of their catch. Their big rough hands were dirty with black grime under their nails.

We had gotten our first taste of fishing from Mogi and Aunt Mary. For them, it was a clever way of distracting six kids for a prolonged period. Across the street from Mogi's old white house were some houses located right along the channel. We had permission from the homeowners to sit on their decks and fish. We would line up like the Von Trapp family, and Mogi and Aunt Mary would give us long cane poles with very specific instructions.

The hook had to be stuck to the bottom of the pole while you were walking so you didn't accidentally cut anyone with it. Once we sat down on the pier next to the channel, we baited our hooks. In our early years, we used your basic white bread balls for bait. Mogi showed us how to dig for night crawlers, but Grandpa Carl bought us bait from the bait shop. That was big time fishing.

Back when we were using white bread, we'd ball it and put it on the sharp end of the hook, press it hard, and lower it into the water until the red and white bobber floated gently on top of the water. Then we'd just sit there and wait.

There was no talking, as that would scare the fish away, though I think this was another trick Aunt Mary and Mogi developed for keeping us quiet. So there we all were, sitting by the channel, hands on our poles, waiting for that bobber to disappear. You had to watch carefully—the fish ran in schools and they could steal your bait if you weren't quick enough. The other tricky thing was not to get your line tangled with anyone else's. Untangling fishing line is a very tedious and time-consuming process, as each of us learned early on.

After what seemed like hours of silence, which never occurred any other time the six of us were together, someone got a nibble. A nibble was when the fish just tasted the bait, like an appetizer, not committed to the whole ball. You didn't pull your line when they were nibbling, only when they went for the whole ball, and then the entire bobber would go under water. As soon as you saw that happen, you had to gently jerk the pole to catch the fish's mouth on the hook and bring him in. If you jerked too fast or too soon, you could lose your bait, fish, or both.

I remember how excited I was when I caught my first fish, pulled it in, and took it off the hook all by myself. It was a bluegill, about three or four inches long. The rule in our family was: YOU CATCH IT, YOU CLEAN IT, YOU EAT IT. I carefully took the fish off the line, holding my hand firmly over its head and restricting the movement of its gills. The gills could cut your hand bad if you didn't hold the fish just right. I started to move the hook out of the fish's mouth while it was wiggling its tail and trying to escape. If it was under two inches it wasn't a keeper—I would have to throw it back. Years later, when we started bringing our boyfriends and girlfriends around, the adults would signal their approval by saying whether or not they were keepers.

Whatever fish we'd catch would go into a bucket of channel water. Once we got back to Mogi's, the cleaning process would begin. First, you had to scale the fish, which consisted of using a knife or scaler, and rubbing it against the scales. On an old stained wooden board, we would cut off the fishes' heads, cut them down the middle, strip out the guts, and cut the tails off. Then we'd rinse them and put them into an empty two-quart milk carton with the top cut off. If we had more fish than we could eat, Mogi would fill the carton up with water and freeze it with the fish in it.

Mogi would let the fish we were going to eat that day sit in milk until she dipped them into breading and fried them until they were crunchy. She served them with homemade Tarter sauce. I think fishing was one of Mogi's ways of teaching us independence.

I once committed the sin of all fishing sins when Mogi specifically told us not to catch a snapping turtle and I did. How was I supposed to avoid it? Put a note on my bread ball that said "Go away, snapping turtles"? When I ran to tell Mogi what happened, she gave me a look that told me I was in for it. She grabbed her tackle box and followed me over to the channel where my brothers were still laughing about what had happened. She got her pliers, snapped the line with the turtle on it, took the line and turtle, and threw it back into the channel. Then she taught me how to put a new sinker and hook on the line and said if I did it again I was on my own.

Another time, over dinner in her garage, Aunt Mary told us, "The first kids who are up early and at my house tomorrow morning will get two dollars to rent a row boat for the whole day—and you don't have to share it with anyone if you don't want to." The challenge had been laid down, and my brothers and sisters and I could get pretty competitive about these types of things. As we began to leave the garage, Aunt Mary mentioned one more thing.

"I'll put those two dollars right here in the red ashtray on the middle of the table. No need to be pounding on my door early in the morning. Come in quiet and don't wake the neighborhood."

That night, John and I devised a plan for getting the two-dollar prize. It meant we were going to have to get up really early, before anyone else, and walk the five miles from Grandpa Carl's pink house to Aunt Mary's.

We'd conspired with Mogi to wake us both up. When we were up and heading out the door, she said, "You two know how to get there now, don't you?" We both nodded yes.

"Be extra quiet when you get to Aunt Mary's, she's not a morning person." We nodded our heads again and went quietly out the back door, holding it carefully so it didn't make a sound when it closed. Mogi stood and watched us as we walked around the side of the house and onto the road. I think she was proud of us.

It was a long walk. Not many people were up and dressed at that hour around Lake Wawasee. It was my first time discovering this part of town by foot. Some of the kitchen lights were on as we passed. All the neatly mowed lawns were covered with heavy morning dew. We boasted about the good job we did getting up early and escaping quietly. The road was wide and John and I walked right down the middle of it with pride. It finally curved around on the other side of pagoda and we knew we were almost there.

John and I passed Bubs and Danny's small dark cottage. The curtains were tightly drawn and the old white pickup truck was in the driveway. They had probably stayed over at Aunt Mary's late, drinking. We found the two dollars in the red ashtray, right where Aunt Mary said it would be, and raced down the gravel path to the bait shop. The man working there took our two dollars with his dirty fingernails and pointed to the pier where the rowboat was tied up. He handed us two oars and gave us specific instructions on where we could go and how much the oars would cost if we lost them.

John and I ran to the boat and untied the rope, placed the wooden oars in their holes, and set off for a day of adventure. We had a boat all to ourselves and we could go anywhere we wanted—pretty much. There were many small channels divided by big bunches of dense lily pads. The channels were so much fun to row around in, and we pretended we were pirates looking for lost treasure. We took turns rowing or we just put the oars in the boat and float if we got tired. The peace and quiet of not being told what to do was amazing.

After about three hours, we docked the boat on the channel closest to Aunt Mary's house. We tied it up real careful. Good thing I had just gotten my rope-tying badge in Girl Scouts that summer. We walked between the two houses across the road toward Aunt Mary's garage. The plan was to get some fishing gear and lunch. We opened the screen door and there was Aunt Mary in her housecoat, sitting there like a lady shouldn't, drinking her coffee and having a cigarette. By that time the rest of our siblings were there and wanted a ride in our boat, and nothing ever felt so good as telling every single one of them no.

Aunt Mary's steel blue eyes locked in on John's and mine, and without her saying a word, we knew we had pleased her. We were beaming with the sense of accomplishment as we packed sandwiches and cookies for our afternoon excursion. As we headed toward the door, Aunt Mary looked over at us. "Why don't you two help yourself to a pop out of the machine." This was the final blessing. She had a big pop machine in her garage that was by invitation-only. We lifted the lid and pulled out a couple of Orange Crush bottles. We used the bottle cap remover on the side of the machine to pop the caps. John and I set off for an afternoon of fishing, eating, and whatever else we felt like doing without asking anyone.

The grand finale of fishing lessons was when I went to visit Aunt Mary in Sarasota, Florida, where she owned another plot of land. She had two houses there, too, one for her and one for Mogi. There was a big trailer set back from both houses that was for company they didn't want in their homes. Aunt Mary built what she called a squirrel room, which I thought she had for the people she entertained, but it actually was to keep the squirrels out. This huge square room had screens for walls, and it was where she and Mogi cooked and entertained. If Mogi or Aunt Mary were in their separate houses, you left them alone, but if anyone was in the squirrel room it meant they were ready to drink, eat, talk, or play cards.

Aunt Mary had a small speedboat at the dock of that Florida house. At night before she went to bed, she would take the leftover crawfish from fishing that day and hang them on a couple fishing poles and leave them dangling at the dock to see what she might catch. Sure enough, the next morning there would always be big ugly catfish on each line she had baited. She said those catfish were dumb and ugly. You had to be extra careful taking catfish off the line because they could sting you with their stingers. Aunt Mary would take them off the hooks, throw them into a bucket of lake water, and bring them up to the squirrel room. She had a long wooden table built to accommodate her size, and this is where she taught me to prepare catfish.

If you have a weak stomach, you should probably skip

to the last paragraph, because this is how it went: First, you had to take a hammer and a two-inch nail and drive the nail through the catfish's head. You didn't want to kill it before you skinned it. When you kill a catfish, it excretes a toxin into its body that will make it taste sour. Who knows how people figure this stuff out? After you're sure the fish is secured by the nail, you take pliers and pull the skin from the head toward the tail. Then, finally, you hit the fish in the head and finish him off. You cut the head and tail off, gut the fish, and soak it in milk until you're ready to fry it up, coated in cornmeal. These fish do make good eating.

When I think back on my fishing days at Lake Wawasee, and later in Sarasota, I remember feeling a deep sense of self-competence. We were learning how to take care of ourselves, to be independent, and that being quiet for a long period catches more than fish.

The Aqua Center

11

The Aqua Center

"We're running away, pack your swimsuit and a towel."
—Kerry

*O*nly one place in Park Forest could bring relief from the ninety-five degree, ninety-five percent humidity in August: The Aqua Center. It was a three-mile walk from 335, and we were free to go as soon as our housework was checked and approved by Charlene. Usually Helen, John, Kerry, and I would depart around the same time with our rolled towels under our arms. Opening day every summer, we spent the entire day at the Aqua Center, coming home with bright red sizzling bodies that didn't really start stinging until we got into bed.

If there was sunscreen back then, we never heard of it, or we couldn't afford it. I loved the coolness of Dermassage, the clean-smelling lotion my mother brought home free from the hospital where she worked. As she squirted it on my back, it immediately turned watery, colliding against the heat of my sunburn. It felt like Mom wore a frozen glove as she rubbed the lotion into my skin. The feel of the evening summer breeze coming through my bedroom window against the coolness of the lotion gave me goose bumps. Then I would head back to the Aqua Center the very next day and every day after to enjoy the freedom to swim and just to be.

There were five pools at the Aqua Center, including the adult pool where absolutely no children were allowed for any reason, and the teenage pool. To gain entry to the badge pool, you had to swim the length of it without sinking, which earned you your badge. At our house you had to sew the badge on yourself. Obtaining it meant freedom from all the younger kids in the toddler pool and a chance to hang around the older, cool kids. The wading pool was where babies could sit and splash with their mothers next to them. All of this was surrounded by the sun deck, a huge, long slab of cement that filled up with an array of bodies in all shapes, sizes, and ages.

Every day during summer, my sisters and I would go through the turnstiles and show our passes, which displayed our names and photos of us smiling with our summer pixie haircuts. We ran through the dressing rooms, pulling off our clothes as quickly as possible, our bathing suits already on underneath. We had to stop and rinse off before entering the pool area, and there were signs everywhere demanding that we walk, not run. Just moments away from the relief of cool chlorinated water, we'd throw our towels onto the low silver wire fence that surrounded the deck and jump into the blue oasis, bobbing with an assortment of colorful bathing caps.

After the initial cool down, we would play all afternoon in the water, competing for who had the straightest handstand, and then who could hold it the longest. Several hours later, Helen, Kerry, and I would grab our towels and lay out on the sundeck. The groove around our faces from our bathing caps stayed long after we took them off. We would slather coconut oil all over our bodies so that we could be among the first in Park Forest to have a rich Hawaiian tan.

After we baked for a while, it was time to buy ice cream at the snack shack. They had the best vanilla and chocolate ice cream, wrapped in a crunchy sugar cone. It was frozen hard, so you could take your time eating it and not worry about it dripping all over. I usually had either a vanilla cone or an ice cream sandwich. I'd lick the ice cream from all around the chocolate cookies, and then bite away the cookie part, then start the whole process again, until all that was left was a small, quarter-sized piece that I'd polish off in one bite.

Sometimes we'd have a dime to buy these treats, but most of the time we didn't. That's when we would collectively pull off a caper. We'd sit on our towels and watch as nearby sunbathers packed all their belongings into their beach bags, including their wallets. They were heading toward the pool, so chances were they'd be gone for a while. I was the lookout while Kerry would go through their bags, get their wallets, grab the money, and put everything back just as it was. Helen would just sit there in her one-piece flowered swimsuit with the ruffles around the hips and look as innocent as she was. After we stole the money, we'd move our towels onto the other side of the sun deck, get settled, and then go buy our ice cream.

As I got older, and Kerry stopped coming around the Aqua Center, I took up the role of masterminding the caper while Helen was on the lookout.

The summer before Dad left, when I was seven and Kerry ten, she woke me up early one morning and said, "I hate it here—and I hate them. We're running away. Pack your swim suit and a towel."

Things at home were escalating already by that point. Mom had already resumed her work as a full time private-duty nurse about a month before my dad left. She was working nights and sleeping during the days. She would often leave a grocery list with a check for Charlene to go shopping. Charlene could stretch a dollar further than anyone, and Dad couldn't hold a candle to her thriftiness.

Since Dad wasn't working at the time, he decided one morning that he'd do the shopping for her.

Dad came home with bags of groceries filled with expensive stuff we were never allowed to eat. Helen, John, and I took one look at the groceries and started to unpack them as fast as we could for fear of my mother waking up before we were done. There was Sugar Frosted Flakes instead of the boring Wheaties and Cheerios; Whip and Chill, a fast delicious pudding, instead of Jell-O. There was only one bag left to unpack when we saw Mom rounding the corner to go to the bathroom. There was dead silence in the kitchen and we all stared at the floor as Mom's eyes assessed the loot and her blurry but intense gaze locked onto Dad's hopeful blue eyes. He slumped forward as he turned his head toward her.

"Milt, what were you thinking? These have to last us two weeks. Put everything back into the bags and return the groceries. Charlene will go to the store with you."

She glanced over at us, indicating with her look that we should start repacking the bounty. All the "good stuff" had to go back. I felt sad that we weren't going to get to eat any of it. For a brief moment it seemed like Dad was like one of us instead of the dad.

Kerry had already put some things into a small suitcase. I didn't give it much thought. It sounded like an adventure. I'd seen children run away on TV and it looked like it could be fun. It generally ended in a good way in the shows I'd seen.

I packed quietly, and we climbed out the bedroom window. We ran down Indianwood, looking behind us, hoping no one would see or catch us. We went to the Park Forest Plaza and stopped at Burnie Brothers Bakery. It was an expensive bakery to us, since we rarely bought baked goods and rarely had any money.

I followed Kerry into the bakery and she asked the price of various items before making her final selections. The lady working behind the counter wore a white frilly apron. She pulled out a pink box, assembled it, and put four fancy cherry and apple turnovers topped with powdered sugar into the box. Kerry said we could eat small pieces of the turnovers so they'd last us at least a week, if not longer. As the lady tied the box closed with string, Kerry pulled her pop bottle money out of her pocket and paid. We headed toward the Aqua Center, which was just a block away from

The Plaza. It opened at ten, so we had plenty of time to create our new home in the woods.

Kerry held the pink box as she talked about her plans for us. "We'll live in the woods across the street from the Aqua Center. We can swim all day, and then sleep in the woods at night. It's better than living in that house, getting bossed around all the time and dealing with that bullshit."

I knew what she was talking about, too. I was young, but I knew enough to know what was happening between my mom and dad. Mom was always yelling about money and bills and how could he do this to his kids. We were always very careful about not saying the wrong thing at the wrong time. I never asked for money for Girl Scouts or a field trip for fear of the look my mom would give my dad, and the look my brothers and sisters would give me.

A couple weeks during our last winter together we all had to sleep on the living room floor because the heat bill hadn't been paid. I thought it was fun that we got to roast marshmallows in the fireplace and it wasn't even a camp out. We learned very fast to hide under our beds when men wearing black suits came to the front door and rang our doorbell. If they couldn't hand their letters directly to someone then they couldn't take the house. At least that's what Charlene told us. I wonder what other kid at the age of seven knew the name of their parents' mortgage company. Ours was Draper & Kramer.

I nodded yes to my sister. I was going along with the

program. Baked goods and swimming instead of walking on eggshells around our house. This was a good solution. I was happy. We set up our stuff in the woods, sat down on our blanket, and each ate a piece of the first apple turnover. Kerry neatly rewrapped the string around the box, "We need to save some for dinner."

At ten o'clock, we carefully tucked our things, including the pink box, into a safe place in the woods and headed for the Aqua Center. Since I hadn't gotten my badge yet, we had to go into the toddler pool, which was only four feet at the deepest end. Only a few people were there that early, and they were mostly adults. We played for a while, enjoying our freedom and looking forward to our turnover dinner later, when we caught sight of our dad walking out of the men's locker room wearing his white undershirt and dark trousers.

His six-foot-four, 250-pound body moved forward in a determined fashion. Kerry looked at me and said, "Get down low in the water and stand as close as you can next to the side of the pool, flat as you can. Maybe he won't see us."

We were the only ones in the toddler pool. He walked past us at first, heading toward the badge pool, but then moments later he turned back around and came walking toward us, through the gates into the toddler pool enclosure. He walked to one end of the pool, and we ran to the other. After three times of doing this, he motioned for a lifeguard to jump in and direct us to the ladder leading out of the pool.

My father's neat brown hair was combed straight back, and I stared at the big wide space between his front teeth as he angrily spoke. "Get out of the pool now. We're going home!" The look on his face didn't invite any comments, so we grabbed our towels off the fence, put our flip flops on our feet, and followed him to the front exit. He went through the men's side, and we went through the women's. As we came out the front, I saw the turquoise station wagon parked right in front.

"What were you two thinking? Your mother is a nervous wreck." The station wagon headed past the woods where our pink box was hiding, and then turned toward Indianwood. I was shivering in my towel, partly cold and partly scared. I wondered what would happen to us. As we pulled into the driveway, my dad turned around and looked at Kerry. "You should know better," he scolded. "Both of you go inside and change, then get in the kitchen. Your mother and I want to talk to you."

Before we could finish dressing, my mother was standing in the doorway of our room with her hands on her hips. Her thick brown hair was fluffy and hugging her neck. All I could see was her bright red lipstick as she declared our punishment. "No one runs away from our home. You're both going to get a beating. Once you're done getting dressed, go to the garage. Your father is waiting."

Kerry glared at our mother as she turned her back on her and headed toward the kitchen. Kerry looked at me, and grabbed some thick storybooks from our bookshelf. "Put two of these in your pants so that when he hits you with the belt, it won't hurt." I did as she said, but there was such a big bulge where my small butt was that I was sure he would notice. We took as long as we could, moving ever so slowly through the kitchen, into the spare room, and through the door into the garage.

Dad was standing there with his belt in hand. "Amy, come here. Do you understand that what you did was bad and that you should never run away?"

I shook my head and started to cry. I was scared.

"Turn around, and lean against the wall."

He held his thick black belt and hit me twice on the butt. "Now, go inside and eat breakfast." As I walked back through the garage door, I took the books out of my pants and put them on top of the long freezer in the spare room. As the garage door closed, I heard my dad say, "Kerry, don't ever do this again, and don't take your little sister with you. Now, you have to take one of those books out of your pants."

I walked into the kitchen with tears running down my cheeks. My mother was standing at the sink with her apron tied around her waist. "Amy, there's Cheerios and a half banana for breakfast. When you're done, clear your place. You'll be spending the rest of this sunny day in your room while your brothers and sisters enjoy themselves at the Aqua Center. What do you have to say for yourself?"

"I'm sorry I ran away. I won't do it again."

What I was really sorry about, though, were those pastries in the pink box sitting in the woods. What would happen to them?

The Peele Kids and Friends

12

Debt

"That Milton, he changes jobs more than I change my under-wear."

—Gogi

"He went out for a loaf of bread, and never came back." That was what my mother said about my father leaving us. There was never any other talk of him or when he might come back—if ever.

I remember overhearing a conversation between my mother and someone on the phone. "Milton thinks he's going to bring the kids to court and make them choose between us." There was silence, and then Mom responded, "Yeah, umm... you're right. He hasn't kept a job for more than a year. The judge will never grant him custody, especially if I bring in that business with the racetrack. He's not going to see any of those kids until he pays me child support."

But he never did pay child support, so we never went to court to choose, and we never saw him. He was out of our lives.

His leaving made me hurt inside, and I quietly cried myself to sleep most nights after he left. But in the mornings it was back to our life of chores and playing and fighting with each other. And dealing with the upset of knowing that Mom worked too hard, owed too many bills, and that we never had enough money.

On the day the men in the black suits came looking for their money, Mom's face was pale as paste and her eyes were wider than usual. She'd been out in the backyard talking to them for a long time. I smiled at them as they walked toward their big fancy car, but their mean stares caused me to look down at my scuffed-up tennis shoes. By the time I looked up, Mom was standing in the front yard yelling our names, her voice shaky, "Bob, Charlene, Kerry, John, Amy, Helen—in the house."

Someone must have done something wrong, At least I knew it wasn't me this time.

Mom was making a phone call by the time we wandered through the front door. After she hung up, she told us to go pee and then get in the station wagon. After a stop at the little Jewel food store, we headed south down Sauk Trail. She repeatedly glanced in he rearview mirror, until finally her frown began to disappear. A lush forest of autumn trees hugged both sides of the narrow two-lane passage. We were taking a trip to the forest preserves, a rare but magical treat.

Mom rolled down her window and cool air flooded in. "Do you smell that, kids?" She took a deep breath in and exhaled. "It's fall and it's time to find that secret Indian trail. The first one out and back gets their pick of the biggest caramel apple."

We already had the doors open by the time she pulled into the parking lot of Sauk Trail Woods. The forest preserves was a dense collection of trees that extended five miles long and three miles wide. Small rock circles formed barbeque pits, perfect fireplaces to roast marshmallows for s'mores. Pathways weaved in and out, marked carefully by scouting projects. A small creek divided the woods, providing a border that let us know when it was time to follow the trail the opposite direction.

"You kids be careful. I'll be waiting for you under the shelter with your caramel apples when you get back."

The shelter was framed with large rocks and there were several picnic tables inside. I picked a small pathway and Helen, then six, followed right behind me. We were surrounded by forest music, a chorus of crunchy sounds of leaves under our feet, and bird conversations above. The bright reds and yellows of the leaves brought a quiet peacefulness to my soul. It was as if God put his big autumn arms around me. I knew I was safe.

"Watch out for the poison ivy, Helen. If you touch it you'll get a horrible rash and it itches bad. Stay on the path and you'll be fine," I always reminded her.

I walked behind to make sure she stayed on the trail. Squirrels scurried up the trees and rolly polly bugs crawled as we navigated our way to the creek. I could hear my brothers off in the forest. I ran up to Helen and whispered in her ear, "Hurry up and let's be the first ones back, what do you say?" Helen nodded and we cut through the brush and circled back on a parallel path heading toward the shelter.

We stopped occasionally to pick up brightly colored orange, red, and yellow leaves to iron between wax paper once we got home. Oddly shaped rocks and acorns beckoned me to take them home as well, making their way into my jacket pockets.

"There's a maple tree and here's some goldenrod," Helen declared, showing off the skills she'd learned in her Brownie troop. Time seemed to disappear as the magic of the forest engulfed us. Huge maple leaves floated down and gently settled on the ground among their colorful neighbors. Being in the forest allowed me to clear my thoughts of the men in the black suits. Sauk Trail Woods was familiar, and I felt safe here.

The path brought us out into a field across from the shelter where we could see our brothers and sisters sitting on the ledge eating their apples. Kerry yelled out, "It's too late, there's none left for you two slow pokes! We ate them all!"

She turned to my other siblings who mumbled, "Yeah, sure was good. Too bad you missed out." Helen started to whine, "Mom, are there any left?"

Mom sat at a picnic table sketching on her artist's pad. "That's enough from all of you," she said as we ran up to her. "Here's your apples, Amy and Helen. Stay away from your brothers and sisters—they'll torture you. When you're both done, we'll head back."

When I peeled the white paper doily off the bottom of the caramel apple, it left an imprint on the bottom and small bits of peanuts trickled on the ground. I licked what remained from the paper before I threw it away. I sat close to my mom as I slowly enjoyed my apple. I bit into the thick caramel and then into the crisp red apple, juice dripping down the side of my mouth. I finished the apple down to the core, slipped the core off the stick, and threw it into the forest yelling, "Grow another apple tree!"

Mom was absorbed in her drawing, so we entertained ourselves by building tall piles of leaves and jumping into them. We took turns seeing who could kick the leaves up into the air, falling flat on our butts and laughing. Bob tackled John too hard and he started crying. Mom looked up, "All right, it's time to go. We'll stop by the Laportes for dinner and then it's home. You have school tomorrow."

Mom had taken care of Frankie LaPorte when she was working at St. James Hospital in Chicago Heights. There was no intensive care unit, so critical patients and rich people had to have private-duty nurses. Frankie was a famous mafia guy—his picture was actually part of a mob family tree we saw in *Life* magazine. He told us our mom was the best nurse ever, and he always paid her in cash.

The LaPorte family had a big home in the South Heights and they did something no other friends of my Mom ever did: They invited our whole family over for Sunday dinner on occasion. The big round women greeted us with warm hugs and filled our plates with pasta, sausages, and garlic bread. There was plenty of food left, even after we all had seconds.

Once we arrived, Mom sat next to Frankie and they started talking. He leaned close to her and it looked like she was telling him a secret. Mom's jaw looked tense, her forehead wrinkled. I looked around at the rest of the people, and everyone was busy laughing and eating. No one seemed to notice that I was watching, here or at home.

After dinner, the biggest round lady put out dessert: fancy bakery cookies and a funny colored ice cream they called spumoni. It was okay, but not as good as the Dairy Queen. I took some cookies and moved myself closer to Frankie and Mom so I could hear what they were saying.

"Frankie, they said they were from Chicago and if I didn't tell them where Milt was that me and the kids were in danger. He owes them some money from a gambling debt. I had no idea."

"Helen, I can't get in the middle of this. Best I can offer is to make a few calls and see if I can ask them to give you some time. These people are not to be taken lightly. Do you know how much he's into them for?"

"A couple thousand dollars." My mother's voice started to get loud and a few of the ladies turned to look. She continued in a softer voice, "I can barely pay the bills. As it is, I can just make the mortgage payment and keep food on the table. I would sure appreciate it if you could at least ask them to give me a few weeks so I can try to find Milt or see if I can borrow some money."

Frankie leaned in, his face looked serious, "I can buy you time, but when they come back to the house you'll need to give them something. See if you can find that husband of yours and tell him he needs to come up with the dough one way or another."

He gave Mom a hug and slipped something into her palm. She tried to hand it back to him, but he waved his hand at her. "Get some groceries for those kids. Take care now."

Mom gave us the time-to-leave sign, and we thanked Mr. LaPorte and his wife for dinner and piled into the car. We were silent on the drive home. The sunset spread a hue of orange with a tinge of red.

That evening, as I sat on the couch in the living room waiting for my turn to shower, I could hear Mom on the phone with Mogi, and then with Aunt Mary. After she hung up I heard Bob ask Mom what Aunt Mary had said. "God Bless Aunt Mary," my mother said. "She said she'd send me a check to cover this month's mortgage, but she won't pay off your father's debt. I'll make some calls tomorrow after work. Don't worry, we'll get through this. We always manage."

When Helen and I were in bed, Mom came in to give us a kiss goodnight. I hugged her, and feeling proud I said, "I polished your nurse's shoes for you, Mom. They're on top of the dryer."

"Thanks honey. You get some sleep now. Good night little Helen."

"Night, Mom. I love you."

"I love you, too." I could hear the racket in the next room. Mom called out, "Kerry and Charlene, stop bickering and get ready for bed. For God's sake, do you ever stop?" Mom left us and walked into their room.

"Kerry took my good sweater, wore it without asking,

and threw it on the floor. I've had it with her touching my things!" Char screamed.

Kerry yelled back, "Shove it up your ass, Char. It's just a stupid sweater for Christ's sake."

"That's it. I'm closing the bedroom door and you two can fight all you want," Mom said.

The door slammed and something hit the adjoining bedroom wall. Mom ignored it, went into her bedroom, and closed the door.

A week later, the men in the black suits came back. After knocking on the front door with no answer, they walked around to the back of the house where Mom was gardening. I was in the back bathroom with the window open, so I could hear their deep strong voices.

"Hello, Mrs. Peele. I think you know why we're here."

"I have no idea where my husband is," Mom said. "He's gone and I'm in the process of filing for a divorce. I'm working six to seven days a week to pay the bills and this house payment." Her voice sounded tired.

"Those all your kids out front, lady?"

"Yes, and don't you dare lay a hand on them." Mom's voice was loud and firm.

"Lady, you got your hands full. If you do hear from that no-good husband, better tell him to watch his back. We'll get our money one way or another." They walked back to their car just as John was climbing up the big oak tree in front of the house.

Kerry was screaming at the top of her lungs. "Get down from that tree or you're dead meat, buddy." John hopped from the top tree branch to the roof laughing and pointing at her. I knew how this would end. Kerry would slam the door and go inside and John would eventually come down from the roof and forget the entire incident. Then Kerry would come after him and they would start the whole thing all over again.

I turned around to watch as the men drove away looking at each other with their heads shaking. I ran around the side of the house, "Mom, Kerry's going to beat up John again."

She looked up from the garden, her eyes puffy and wet, "John knows enough to stay up there until Kerry gives up. Go play, honey."

I looked at Mom. "Are we in trouble with those mean men?"

"No honey, they just needed some of our money and we can't give them any. We're in debt up to our eyeballs, but we're all together and that's what's more important than all the money in the world."

I hugged her and went back to watch the John and Kerry show, which provided an easy distraction from Mom's adult issues that I wasn't old enough to fully understand, and which scared me because of how much they scared her.

Mom, Amy, and Helen

13

Penny Candy

"We were going to be rich."
—Amy and Helen

After a full morning of swimming, napping, and playing, it was time for Helen and me to strategize about how to make our first big buy of penny candy. The thought of buying mass quantities of candy as soon as possible was what fueled our need to make quick cash. We knew that simply asking for money was not acceptable. Our mother told us repeatedly that we must work hard to earn it, there are no free rides.

There were chores that brought no income, such as making our beds, doing dishes, keeping Mogi's house straightened, and cleaning up after dinner. Allowance was a word we never heard. We had a roof over our heads, so we had better carry our weight. After searching the obvious places for any coins that may have accidentally fallen out of someone's purse or pocket and finding nothing, we started to look through Mogi's cabinets and drawers for anything that looked like something we could sell.

At home we put on shows and circuses in the backyard or garage whenever we could, which would bring in about twenty-five cents. Now, we never actually compared what we spent to put on the show, pop the corn, and then bag and sell it, but we had money at the end. We couldn't run fast enough to the penny candy store two blocks down the street from our house and let the spending begin. I remember the afternoon of my first communion, after I had collected all my cards with checks and money in them. All counted, it was twenty-five dollars, which felt like a million dollars to me at the time. I led my friends down to the penny candy store and let them buy anything they wanted. I felt like the richest girl in the world. I was pretty darn popular for about twenty minutes after that outing.

On Kale Island, Helen and I decided that a good place to start searching for money was in Mogi's drawers. One of us had to look out for Mogi, though, because if she caught us looking through her drawers there would be hell to pay. Opening the drawer brought forth a smell of a cedar chest after it's been closed for a long time. Finding nothing we could possibly try to resell without Mogi noticing, we went out to the screened-in porch and sat down. We were sitting there feeling discouraged when, through the window, Helen noticed a colorful box on a shelf inside the house. She ran in and pulled it off just as Mogi was walking through the screen door. We caught each other's eyes and I saw my own terror mirrored back to me in my little sister's face.

Mogi walked over to Helen and gently took the box from her before sitting down next to her. She gestured for me to sit on the other side as she began to open the box and explain its contents to us.

"This is a potholder kit, girls, and if you'd like I'll show you both how to make one."

My sister and I locked on to each other's eyes. We were going to be rich!

Mogi patiently showed us how to stretch each loop over the metal prong on either side of the loom. She suggested using different colored loops to make a design. After we were done putting the loops on all the metal prongs one way, it was time to begin weaving the loops up and over the opposite way. At first we were clumsy, but we soon began to master the weave. We each had our own loom, and after completing the weaving and tightening of each loop we were ready for Mogi to show us how to take the potholder off the loom. This was tricky, and if done incorrectly you could lose all your work. Mogi got a crochet hook and began to pull one loop through the next until they were all firmly linked around the edges to make a firm border. She pulled the last loop through and showed us how to make the handle of the potholder. We offered our very first potholder to Mogi, which she accepted with pride. Before she was halfway to the kitchen with her new gift, we started in on our next one.

Before we knew it, we were being called for lunch. We put away our potholders and ran to the table. My brothers had been fishing, so our lunch consisted of fresh lake perch, sliced homegrown tomatoes, and potato salad. We ate as fast as we could, no time for seconds, cleaned up, and raced back to our potholder factory.

We surveyed our colorful potholders and set off to peddle our wares. We had no idea how much to sell one for as we rang the doorbell at one of Mogi's neighbors' houses. A lady as old as Mogi answered at the first house we went to and looked down at us.

"Well, hello girls, what can I do for you?"

Helen and I stared at each other. Finally, I spoke up.

"Would you like to buy a homemade potholder, Ma'am?" We shuffled back and forth, trying hard not to feel like we were begging. Then she popped the question.

"How much for two of them?" She had selected our two best ones. It was clear she knew her potholders. Helen and I looked innocently into her eyes. She sensed our discomfort with closing the sale and offered a price.

"How about I give you each a quarter—one for each potholder? Did you girls actually make these yourself?" Helen and I could not believe our ears—twenty-five cents! We were going to have to open a savings account if this kept up. Helen responded quickly, keeping her eyes trained on the lady opening her black satin coin purse with a single small clasp in the middle.

"My sister and I just learned how to make them today from our grandmother."

"Who's your grandmother?"

I replied, "Lillian Kurtzfield, she lives in the white two-story house over there." I turned and pointed toward Mogi's house.

The woman took two quarters out of her purse and placed one gently into each of our hands. "You mean the house that has all those wild kids running up and down the road?"

Helen and I looked at each other as we clenched the coin and tucked it into the pocket of our shorts.

"Thank you," we both chimed. We backed away from the doorway and ran as fast as we could down the road toward the penny candy store before she could change her mind. Once in the store, we glanced around to make sure none of our siblings were there. We began the time-consuming task of picking out twenty-five separate pieces of candy.

Slowly skipping back to Mogi's house, we stopped often to open our small white paper bags to view the mountain of gold we'd just purchased. And the best part was that we didn't have to share it with anyone.

My bag had all my favorites: two pretend red lipstick candies, candy buttons on white paper, three root beer barrels, five tubes of mini-chocolate balls that crunched when you ate them, four caramels with the white swirls, and two atomic fireballs. I decided to start with the lipstick. Helen lagged behind, slowly assessing her stash. We decided to walk over to the channel to quietly sit and slowly enjoy our feast.

That summer Helen and I really thought we could have made at least a million dollars. By the end of summer almost every house and cottage on Kale Island had their own handmade potholders. And Helen and I decided to wait until the next summer to open our savings account.

Helen, Amy, Kerry, and Charlene

14

Goldblatt's

"You got yourselves into this mess, and you should get your-selves out."

—Mom

It was a cool fall Saturday morning in Park Forest, Illinois. The leaves had just started to turn from green into hints of red and orange with tips of yellow. I was ten and Kerry was thirteen. Kerry usually took me with her on her capers, since Charlene would never consider dragging me along for anything. I did whatever Kerry said. I had to, or else she would beat me up.

Charlene had finished checking my chores, which was the bathroom on this particular day. I had scrubbed the tub, sink, and toilet with generic cleanser. I hated to wash the toilet. We had only one bathroom and it was always dirty, especially with two boys. But in order to pass inspection, the bathroom had to be immaculate. By the time I called Charlene for inspection, the chrome along the sink and tub was polished and shining, and I was always especially proud of that. The brown tile floor was washed by hand and dried with a towel. The mirror was sparkling clean and fresh towels hung from the bar on the wall.

"I'm ready for you to check the bathroom," I yelled out to Charlene. When she came in, I watched her eyes as she looked from the toilet to the sink and then the tub. She even picked up the white cap that lay beside the bottom of the toilet to make sure I had washed under and around it.

"Looks good, you can go out now," she informed me. "Where are you going?"

Before I could answer her, Kerry popped up from behind Charlene, looking around her shoulder.

"Amy and I are going down to The Plaza," she interrupted.

Char knew better than to expect more information from Kerry. She never was much for words, and she thought everyone should mind their own god damn business. Charlene looked her square in the eye. "You two don't have any money to go shopping, what are you going to do there?"

Kerry walked down the hall to our bedroom, "We can window shop and you can't stop us!" Charlene just shook her head. Sometimes it was all she could do to ignore Kerry.

Sometimes they would get into knock down drag out fights with hair pulling and lots of swear words. Kerry had been angry since our dad left, and she was mean most of the time.

We walked out the screen door and crossed the front lawn that John had just mowed. Blades of fresh cut grass stuck to the sides of our sandals. We made our way toward The Plaza, which was two long blocks from our house.

I looked at Kerry, "Which store are we going to, Marshall Fields?" I loved their Barbie Doll clothes collection.

"You know we're too poor to walk into that place. We're going to Kresge's for some fries and then I want to go over to Goldblatt's to look around." Sounded just fine to me.

Kresge's was our five and dime and it had the second best soda counter at The Plaza, after the Grill. We slid into the red booth and a waitress in a frilly white apron and short black dress came up. "What do you girls want?"

Kerry took her babysitting money out of her pocket, "We'll have a large order of fries and a cherry Coke."

"You both have to order something or you can't sit in a booth." Kerry gave her one of her mean looks, raising one eyebrow. "Then give her a cherry Coke, too."

"I want a vanilla Coke."

The waitress turned on one heel and went to place our order. Kerry gave out a loud sigh, "What a bitch." I cringed, hoping the waitress hadn't heard. I didn't want to get thrown out. I wondered if the waitress knew how poor we were.

After we enjoyed every last crunchy fry and a fair amount of free catsup, Kerry got up and nodded for me to follow her.

We went up and down different aisles and looked at hair products, empty photo albums, cheap clothes, make-up, and then turned down to my favorite aisle, the candy aisle. At that moment, Kerry whipped around and grabbed my blouse. She whispered, "Look, just pick one or two candy bars you want and quickly shove them down your shorts. Then we're getting the hell out of here."

I was scared, but I didn't have any money and I wanted some candy. I grabbed a five-cent Butterfinger and a few Reese's peanut butter cups and shoved them in my shorts. My heart was racing and my eyes were darting all over the place. I knew I was doing something wrong, but it was exciting, too.

Kerry grabbed my arm, "Just look normal and slowly walk toward the door. Stop and look at something right by the door, then slowly walk out like you got all the time in the world."

Good thing she told me that or I would have run out the door and surely given myself away. A few stores past Kresge's, I went to take the candy from my pants but Kerry stopped me. "Not yet, wait till we turn the corner, in case anyone's looking."

The candy was wedged in the elastic band of my shorts. "They're digging into my skin," I complained.

"Shut up, you big baby, we're almost out of sight."

A few minutes later, I was enjoying my Butterfinger. I opened the Reese's peanut butter cups and gave Kerry one. We strolled past Fannie May's Candy—that was for the real rich people. We passed the Holiday Theater and then walked into Goldblatt's, candy and wrappers long gone. I followed Kerry to the record area and watched as she started flipping through the forty-fives. I knew she didn't have any money, but I figured she was just browsing. Next thing I knew she took a stack of forty-fives and shoved them down the front of her pants, grabbed my arm, and started for the door. I shook my arm free and kept pace with her until we got right in front of the double doors to leave. Then I stopped.

Kerry looked at me with her gritted teeth, "Amy, come on now, we have to go!"

I looked at her smugly, "You got to look around. I want to look at these wallets." I picked up a black leather one. It was soft, with lots of room for pictures and a little clip coin purse attached to it.

Kerry's voice got louder, "We're leaving now!" I looked at her red face, put down the wallet, and followed her outside.

As we started to walk toward Sears, a lady called after us, "Excuse me girls, could you please wait a minute?" Kerry slowed down and glared at me as she turned around. There was no mistaking that look—she was going to kill me. "You are dead meat, sister," she said.

It was Marie, the store detective. Everyone knew her and she was a running joke. She was five-foot-two and wore a tan raincoat even when it wasn't raining. She wore old lady black shoes and carried a black handbag that was almost as big as she was. You could spot her a mile away, but we hadn't.

She walked up to Kerry, "Young lady, do you have something that doesn't belong to you?" Kerry was quick to reply, "No!"

"I think you do. Now follow me back into the store and I won't call the police. We can keep this as store business."

I looked at Kerry, who started to follow Marie back into the store. I followed, my heart pounding so loud I thought everyone could hear it. Marie took us behind a curtain marked "Employees Only" and into a small room with a gray metal desk. She closed the door behind us.

"Now, what's under your shirt?"

Kerry took the records out and threw them on the desk. I couldn't believe she was acting like this. We were in enough trouble already and her being rude was only going to make things worse. We were in serious trouble. Marie looked Kerry straight in the face. "How often do you two girls steal here?"

Kerry let out a huff. "We've never stolen anything here before."

"How can I believe you? If you steal, you probably lie too."

"Believe anything you want. I don't give a damn."

Marie was angry now. "That's it, I'm calling your parents, and I may even call the police. What's your name?"

Kerry calmly looked at Marie and said, "Carol Wright." I couldn't believe she was lying. We were getting deeper in by the minute.

"What's your phone number?"

"PI 8-7864."

Marie picked up the phone and dialed. A man's voice answered.

"Hello, this is Marie from down at Goldblatt's. I'm sorry to tell you we have your daughter Carol here for shoplifting." A pause.

Marie slammed down the phone. "He doesn't have a daughter!" She looked over at me. "Now you better tell me your real names or I'm calling the police to come pick you both up and we'll see you in court."

Kerry was giving me the don't-spill-it look, but I was only ten and I wasn't good at lying or stealing yet. I blurted out, "My name is Amy Peele and this is my sister Kerry and our number is PI 8-2434."

I could feel Kerry's eyes burning a hole through the side of my head. "Nice job, asshole."

Marie dialed our number and Mom answered the phone. We were screwed.

"Mrs. Peele, this is Marie from Goldblatt's. I'm sorry to have to call you like this, but we have your daughters Kerry and Amy here, and they've been caught shoplifting. I'd rather not call the police. Could you come down here and we can settle this matter here at the store?"

A look of confusion registered on Marie's face as she put the receiver down. "I'm sorry, girls," she said. "Your mother wants me to go ahead and call the police."

I was shocked and scared as I watched Marie dial the Park Forest police department. I looked over at Kerry for some comfort, but she was acting like nothing was wrong. I considered the fact that she had watched too many prison movies and had become numb to the consequences of serious crimes. It seemed like a long time until a uniformed policeman knocked on the door. Marie stepped outside and closed the door behind her. As soon as they left, Kerry leaned over and gave me a knuckle sandwich hard in my left arm. She always made her middle finger knuckle stick out so it stung when she hit, and it always left a bruise on my arm.

"You stupid bitch. If you hadn't told her our names she may have let us go. Now we're really dead, thanks to you. Mom's gonna beat us."

Seconds later, the officer opened the door and gestured for us to follow him. I looked down at the floor the whole way to the police car, hoping no one we knew was in the store. It was already dark out, which meant it was dinnertime. Our brothers and sisters would know about our crime.

The police station was a couple of blocks from The Plaza, and once we arrived we were taken into a big room with a wooden desk and chairs. A short fat balding officer with glasses sat across from us. His badge said "Officer Milky."

"Hello, Kerry and Amy. It seems we have a problem here."

How did he know our names already? Neither of us had said a thing.

"You want to tell me what happened over at Goldblatt's?" I wasn't going to speak. I didn't want a bruise on my other arm. I nodded to Kerry.

"I stole a few forty-fives, big deal."

Officer Milky pulled his chair up to the table and leaned toward us. "It's a very big deal because both of you have a police record now. I've called your mother three times and she has hung up on me each time. She says you got yourselves into this mess and you should get yourselves out. She wants me to keep you here. She doesn't want thieves in her house. I can't say I blame her."

He looked over at me. Tears were beginning to roll down my face. This was the most terrible trouble I had ever gotten into in my life. "Amy, you're a little young to be in jail overnight, don't you think?" I nodded my head and then burst into a full-blown cry. Kerry sat there, not reacting to Office Milky. He handed me a Kleenex box.

"I'll try your mother one more time, but if she doesn't come, then we're going to have to ship you to the Juvenile

Hall in Chicago Heights and you'll spend the night there." He got up and left the room. I looked at Kerry, tears streaming down my face. "This is just great!"

She glared back at me, "Just shut up, they can't send us to Juvenile Hall. Our crime isn't that big."

Officer Milky came in shaking his head. "You two ladies are lucky. Your mom's on her way, but I wouldn't want to be you two when you get home. She is very angry and tired. Too bad she has to work all day and then come home to this kind of news. Shame on both of you! Follow me."

We accompanied him to the front lobby, where he motioned for us to sit on the black vinyl chairs. "Stay there. Your mother will be here in a minute, and don't even think about moving." I watched him go back into the dispatcher's room. When I turned my head, I saw my mother walking into the police station, still dressed in her white nurse's uniform. She walked right past us as if we didn't exist, and turned around to speak to Officer Milky. She seemed to know her way around the station. I realized my brother had probably been here once or twice before.

She came back to where Kerry and I were sitting. "Get in the car," she deadpanned.

We got up and she followed us out. As soon as we left the parking lot she started in. "So, Kerry, you're not content getting into trouble alone. You have to bring your little sister along for the ride now. Amy, where is your common sense? You know better. Shame on both of you for disgracing yourself and our family. It's bad enough your father leaves me with six kids, debt, and no money, but then this shit. I work seven days a week, ten hours a day, just to keep a roof over your heads and food on the table and this is how you show me respect. Well, I've had it! Kerry, I've grounded you, taken away every privilege you have, and you still defy me. This is the last straw!"

She pulled into our driveway and slammed the car into park. "Both of you get inside and go straight to the bathroom." My mother went into the kitchen, opened a drawer, and took something out before catching up with us on our way to the bathroom.

I was trembling. I didn't know what to expect. Kerry had long since detached from my mother's threats and beatings. It seemed like nothing could make her feel remorse. The house was silent. My mother closed the bathroom door and placed a big pair of silver scissors on the sink. "Take off all your clothes. You want to act like criminals, I'm going to treat you that way!"

The rage I felt from my mother was the most intense I'd ever experienced. She was out of control and I was terrified.

She made Kerry stand under the cold shower, and then she began to cut her long brown hair off in clumps. I screamed and screamed for her to stop. She kept cutting. I stood there shivering from fear and cold, scared that I was next and scared for my sister. Would my mother stop at that, or would she do something else even worse?

It took a long time before she was finished. My sister screamed and cried the whole time. My mother turned to me and said, "Next time you two think about stealing something, think of this. Now put your clothes back on, clean up this bathroom, and go to bed."

She left the bathroom. My expectations of what she was going to do to me lessened when I poked my head into the hallway and watched her go into her bedroom, but my fear of what might happen another day was still strong.

I cried myself to sleep that night. The next day, no one mentioned what had happened, and Kerry and I never talked about what happened that night, just like none of us kids ever talked about Dad leaving.

Lake Wawasee

15

Midnight Swim

"You two ready for an adventure?"
—Kerry

Mom backed the turquoise station wagon from the driveway of 335 Indianwood. All six of us kids piled into the car. Bob, now fourteen, claimed a window in the middle seat. Ten-year-old John staked out the opposite window. Char and Kerry settled in the front passenger seat, each hoping to control the radio if Mom was in a good mood. As I was eight and Helen five, squeezing into the middle seat between the boys would be risky at best, so we promptly climbed into the small foldout bench seat in the very back of the car.

We recited our ritual prayer to St. Christopher to give us a safe trip to Mogi's house. We soon forgot God, however, and began comparing each other to roadside cows as we sailed down Route 30. This didn't last too long before we heard the roar of my mother's voice, threatening to turn the car around if we didn't stop immediately. She rarely made idle threats; the only one she never went through with was to drop us off at the orphanage, but that was a close call.

One time she slammed on the brakes, pulled the car over to the side of the road, and made us get out. We all had to line up against the back of the car, bend over, and get a whack across the butt from Dad's long thick black belt—the only thing he left her with when he moved out. The belt hurt, but I was more embarrassed by what the people in the passing cars might be thinking as they sped by. Probably that we were a bunch of unruly kids on our way to a military school. Soon after the dramatic stop, however, we were singing all the verses to "She'll Be Coming Around the Mountain."

At the halfway point, we stopped at a Welco gas station for a potty break and chocolate shakes, made to order. The last hour-and-a-half of the drive seemed like forever. I couldn't wait to plunge into the cleansing waters of Lake Wawasee. When we heard the rumble of the steel grates as we crossed onto Kale Island, we all grew still, as if a maestro had just raised his wand. The sound of the gravel driveway announced we were at Mogi's house and the restraints and orders so heavily present in our everyday life evaporated as soon as I opened the car door. Once us kids headed toward the lake, Mogi and Mom could enjoy their alone time together without interruptions.

I jumped out of the station wagon, hugged Mogi, and ran inside to her bathroom. Careful not to show my naked body to anyone, as Sister Norbert at school said that was a mortal sin, I quickly slipped into my one-piece bathing suit. Leaving my clothes and tennis shoes in a neat pile, I grabbed a beach towel and began the first of many barefoot runs to Kale Beach. I could smell the clean lake before I saw it, and I threw my towel on the white bench. Running to the end of the pier, I jumped through the air as if I had wings, knowing the water would welcome my body and soul with total acceptance. The first dip into Lake Wawasee was delicious. With a splash, I immersed my body into the velvety liquid. The cool water was so clear I could see rocks and shells at the bottom. I always started my first swim with a doggy paddle, and then shifted into freestyle as I heard the rest of my brothers and sisters heading down the pier.

I swam out to the raft, which belonged to all those who were members at Kale Beach. Some used it to sunbathe on, while others—like my siblings and me—played King of the Raft with it. I swam to where the water was deeper and cooler, and dove down to grab a handful of sand. I put the sand on the raft and sifted through it for treasures: a closed mussel, a sparkly rock, shells that were pinkish and smooth inside. When I had enough bounty from my dives, I swam back to shore and started my pile under the white bench, where my treasures would gather all summer long. I'd select the prettiest ones to take home with me.

Froggy was a middle-aged man, very tall at six-foot-four, with skinny legs and a beer belly that hung out past the tight T-shirts he always wore. His house faced the lake and his back door was near the main road. We thought the flashing neon Budweiser sign in his front yard was cool. He and his wife often sat inside and watched us play and swim for hours. The only time we saw him actually move was when he came out to fix something on his pontoon or pier. He was a close friend of Aunt Mary's, which meant she had Camel nonfiltered cigarettes and Budweiser available at her house when he visited. They played poker together. I figured he beat her a lot because she always called him "Goddamn Froggy." He wasn't mean or nice to us kids—he was just there. He and Mrs. Froggy didn't have any kids, only two small yapper dogs. It was hard to believe that not everyone had kids.

Most days at Kale Beach included at least four hours of swimming, along with fishing, renting a two-dollar rowboat for the whole day, and eating. When I went fishing with Mogi, we'd go really early in the morning. When I had money to spend, my trips to the root beer stand for penny candy usually took place after the required lunchtime nap. The evenings rolled around slowly, and if it wasn't my turn to wash, dry, or put away dishes, Helen and I would take the short path down to the neighbors' pagoda to feed the swans. After evening chores and the nightly Dairy Queen, we'd catch as many fireflies as we could and put them in rinsed-out pickle jars with holes punched in the tops. We were so proud of our homemade light bulbs.

It was always nice and quiet in Mogi's house as we slipped between the clean crisp sheets, and I usually fell asleep before my head hit the cool pillow. I never heard my brothers or sisters come in from their evening capers. Our family rule about swimming at night was that you had to be able to swim from the pier to the raft at least four times nonstop without getting winded. That took quite a bit of practice. The actual rules of Kale Beach stated that no one was supposed to swim at night. You could lose your beach permit for the summer if you got caught. But that never stopped me or my siblings from enjoying our night swims.

One night just before bedtime, Kerry came to the room where Helen and I were getting ready for bed and motioned for me to follow her. She was usually up to something. At eleven, she was bigger than us, and we always did what our older sisters said.

"You two ready for an adventure?'

Helen gazed into Kerry's blue eyes.

I spoke up," What kind of adventure?"

"Go out to the clothesline and get your suits, I'm taking you down to the lake." It had been a hot and humid day, and there still wasn't much of a breeze outside. Helen and I ran outside, careful not to let the screen door slam. We grabbed our suits, along with the clothespins that held them up, and ran back into the house.

"Hurry up, just change here. No one's looking."

"I'm not changing in the middle of the living room, someone might walk in." I went into the bathroom.

"Like anyone cares to see your flat chest, Amy. Hurry up, you two!"

Helen changed in front of Kerry, and the three of us snuck out through the front door, careful to make sure none of the adults could see us from Aunt Mary's garage.

Before we got very far, Kerry turned around. "Now don't talk until we get around the corner." We walked silently down the stony road to the beach. In one of the living rooms that faced the road, a man sat in a big La-Z-Boy chair, beer in hand, staring at the television. He never looked our way. After we were far enough down the road, Kerry stopped.

"Listen up, and I'll tell you the deal. Froggy has a motion light at his back door."

Helen's eyebrows curled, "What's a motion light?"

Kerry continued, "When you move, the light goes

on and it signals Froggy that there's a burglar or murderer on his property. He'll get his gun and come out looking. Just follow me, keep your mouth shut, and you'll be fine. Usually, I wait till after ten and then Froggy's too drunk to hear anything."

I felt like a real spy moving slowly and carefully to avoid that light. Once past the Froggy light trap, we had to get in the water quietly, using the steel ladder at the end of the pier to lower ourselves in. The night water was warm, like bath water.

The lights from the houses surrounding the lake sparkled as if there were hundreds of invisible fairies and all you could see were their wands reflecting off the black twinkling sky and the glassy lake. The sound of the waves against the cement wall at the end of the pier was hypnotic. We swam, all the while keeping our joy-filled sounds as hushed as we could, performing handstands and front and backwards somersaults. We didn't worry about the adults back in Aunt Mary's garage coming after any of us. They were too busy drinking and playing cards to notice we were gone.

After we had been in the water for a while, I saw Kerry twirling something around her head. As I swam up to her, she jumped up high and I could see her bare chest exploding out of the water, both white breasts bouncing freely. I let out a scream and started laughing. Froggy clicked on the bright lights in front of his house and came rumbling out slurring,

"Who the hell is out there? I'll call the sheriff if you don't get your goddamn asses out of here now!"

My heart was pounding out of my chest, but we hid perfectly still under the pier. Froggy stayed out there for what seemed like an hour, but he finally turned off the outside light, then his living room light, and went up to bed. There was no way we would let ourselves get caught. We had seen the late-night prison shows and we didn't want to end up there. After we were sure Froggy had passed out upstairs, Kerry motioned for us to come close to her. We were still under the pier, crouched down so just our heads were visible.

"Take off your suits, you'll love it."

I whispered into Kerry's ear. "I'm not taking off my clothes, you know it's a mortal sin. You're going to hell."

Kerry came right up to my face, "Who's feeding you that bullshit?"

"Sister Norbert."

A big smile crossed her face, "It's a mortal sin for nuns: it's only a venial sin for us. I've confessed a million times and didn't even get an extra Hail Mary. Don't be chicken. Just put your suits on top of the pier. I promise I won't steal them."

Kerry swam out from under the pier away from us. I slowly removed my suit, keeping my entire body under the water except for my head. Helen followed my lead. We put our suits in a pile on the pier.

The warm waters of Lake Wawasee coated every inch of my body like liquid satin against my bare skin. My cheeks warm from embarrassment, I looked around and realized no one was watching me. Helen had already started to swim quietly toward Kerry. I moved my body through the water and began to enjoy the freedom and cool sensations of the lake water. I pretended to be a mermaid swimming around and under the pier, or a graceful, delicate ballerina. I swam over to my sisters and we did handstand-somersault routines for each other as we stifled giggles about our naked bodies being exposed to the entire lake.

Finally, after a long time, Kerry swam over to get her suit and Helen and I watched as she dipped it back into the water and put it on. We did the same, but after such freedom—the most freedom I'd ever felt in my life—the suit felt restrictive. Helen and I wrapped our towels around ourselves and slowly followed Kerry around the motion light and down the road. Circles of gnats swarmed in the yellow hue of the streetlights. I took a deep slow breath and felt the smile in my heart fill my entire body.

Beacon

Epilogue

The Will

"Where there's a will, there's a relative."
—Aunt Mary

Mogi died in 1971 of a surgical complication at the age of sixty-seven. Aunt Mary died in 1979 at the age of seventy-two. She passed away at her Florida home from cancer of the pancreas. Her brother Bill's daughter, Linda, was at her bedside. According to Mom, she and Linda discussed the will, but neither one of them had a copy. So Mom left 335 and drove to Kale Island to meet with Aunt Mary's attorney, who informed her he did not have the will. Mom went to Aunt Mary's to find Bubs and Danny in Aunt Mary's house rifling through her desk. Mom walked into the small yellow house and asked, "Bubs and Danny, what are you doing here?"

Danny puffed out his chest and turned toward Mom, "We're here to find the will. Mary told us she was going to leave the property to us." He took a long drag from his cigarette, Bubs was sniffling behind him.

"I think you need to leave until I find it. I'll let you know if she left you anything."

"She left us everything, she told us so before she left for Florida," Bubs insisted, wiping at her eyes with a tissue.

"If that's true I'm sure we'll read it in the will," Mom maintained. "Where's her cash? She always kept at least five hundred on hand."

"Don't have a clue," Danny blurted out. He put his arm around Bubs and they started for the door. Bubs turned around once again and said, "We took care of her most of her life. You didn't have time chasing all the kids. We deserve everything, not you. She gave you all enough while she was alive." Bubs eyes teared up again and she walked outside where Danny helped her into their white pick-up truck and pulled out of the driveway, the tires on his truck squealing as they drove away.

Mom later called each one of us and told us that Aunt Mary had died. Bob was thirty-two, married and living in Springfield with his wife Nancy and son, Brandon. Char, thirty-one, was living in Chicago with her son Jeremy; Kerry, twenty-nine, was living with her daughter Carla in Park Forest; John, twenty-eight, and his wife Elva were in California raising their first child, Elliot. I was twenty-six and single, living in Chicago and working full-time as transplant coordinator at the University of Chicago; and Helen, twenty-three, was married to Ray, living in Monee.

I could hear the sadness in Mom's voice when she called me, even before she told me. Mom called each one of us, laughing and crying as we each reminisced about our favorite Aunt Mary stories.

"How are you doing, Mom?" I asked.

"I'm sad to lose her. She was always there for us. If it weren't for Aunt Mary and Mogi, we would have lost our house several times. They bailed my ass out of more jams. She really loved you kids and there is a piece of her inside of each one of you."

I kept listening as she talked, but my mind was back on Kale Island.

"The lake will always be there for you kids," she said as we hung up the phone. As I put down the receiver, I imagined myself jumping from the end of the pier into the healing waters of Lake Wawasee.

Acknowledgments

I am deeply grateful to my first writing teacher and mentor, Guy Biederman, who compassionately taught me to write one word, sentence, and story at a time. To my writing tribe, Bella Quattro: Betsy Fasbinder, Christie Nelson, and Linda Joy Myers, who held my hand and encouraged me to put duct tape over the loud critic on my shoulder.

To my patient and loving husband who believed in me even when I did not believe in myself, and who became my publisher and photographer for this edition. To my writing coach and editor, Brooke Warner, for her gentle and persistent partnership.

Finally, to my mother, for showing up and raising six independent kids who all thought they were only children. She kept a roof over our heads and taught me forgiveness when she forgave my father for leaving her and us. If it were not for her, I would have never known the healing waters of Lake Wawasee.

About the Author

Amy S. Peele completed a year of improvisational training from Second City in Chicago. After living in Chicago for thirty-one years, she moved to California. Working in the field of transplantation for over thirty years with several major medical centers, she treasures the simple moments life offers. Though Amy's professional publishing history includes several chapters and numerous articles on organ transplantation, she has a penchant for personal writing. In 2003, she published a short story in *Becoming Whole: Writing Your Healing Story*, by Linda Joy Meyers, PhD. With her husband, Mark Schatz, she raised their two children, Gracie and Bennett, in Novato, California, where they still reside.